Understanding the Matthew Effect

Understanding the Matthew Effect

Unlocking the Mystery Behind Why the Rich Get Richer

Mark Wilburn

For general information about our products or services, please visit our website at neoscdg.com, or contact the author at mwilburn@neoscdg.com.

Library of Congress Cataloging-in-Publication Data is on file with the publisher.
Publishers Cataloging-in-Publication Data
Understanding the Matthew Effect; by Mark Wilburn
128 pages cm.
Paperback ISBN: 979-8-9857168-0-1
Ebook ISBN: 979-8-9857168-1-8

Printed in the United States of America

Endorsements

I know Mark Wilburn as a man of God, called according to his purpose to be a spear-header, a fore-runner, and a path-forger to Equip God's people to produce wealth both for themselves and for the Kingdom of God. I know many people who have prospered greatly by gleaning from His revelation knowledge and his stock market system regarding trading. I believe this book, "Understanding the Matthew Effect", is one of the essential stepping stones to releasing all people everywhere from Lack and bringing them into the prosperity that God intended for his children to enjoy. Mark has very artfully described Kingdom concepts in a way that anyone can understand. It is a must-read for anyone desiring to increase their personal wealth.

Nancy Coen
President of Global Ascension Network
Owner, Tree of Life Wellness Center

Transparent, Trustworthy and Teacher.

When I think of Mark WIlburn, that's what I think of! I've learned that whatever I want in life, someone, somewhere has already done it. When it comes to trading the markets, Mark is that person. His skill puts him at a high level, but it's his character that keeps him there! That's why I'm excited about this new book. He dives into the mindsets and secrets that take success to the next level. This is not just a book of abstract thoughts and pithy sayings. It's a practical handbook that you'll refer to again and again! Get ready for your mind to shift and your results to increase!

Dennis McIntee
Leadership Development Group

Mark Wilburn has created a fantastic narrative in the way he has addressed underlying issues within the culture of humanity's thinking regarding financial stewardship. It is a great tool of instruction for people wanting to grasp one of the secrets of YHVH's household and its practical application, to express and experience what it means to shatter the ceiling and reach into what has seemed impossible for most of us.

I found this book convicting and informative at the same time. A challenge to us to get to grips with a subject that YHVH is highlighting as part of the code of our day.

Ian Clayton
International Speaker/Consultant
Son Of Thunder

It is with great joy that I want to encourage you to read this Book. Mark and Kate are dear friends of mine and have four amazing young men they are raising. In all my years of travel and ministry, I have yet to come across a couple who have such a deep and clear understanding of wealth, become wealthier, and generosity. They most certainly are the real deal and live their message.

Their keys, if applied, will steer you into financial wealth and freedom. Mark deals extensively with 'the bottom' line. If these foundations are dealt into, your pathway to financial freedom is sure!

I wholeheartedly endorse *The Matthew Effect* and all subsequent books that follow.

Lindi Masters
Ignite Hubs International

Fun. Inspiring. Provocative. This book is all of these. Mark's insights will spur you to think and envision life differently. And his wit will keep you reading all the way to the end.

Dr. Allen Hunt
Best-Selling Author

"Mark embodies financial integrity. The application of the simple tools presented in this work have the capacity to reshape your financial future while keeping your conscience clear."

Joseph Sturgeon
International Consultant

Dedication

I dedicate this book to my parents. Growing up, you modeled in your lifestyle many of the principles laid out in this book. While you never necessarily taught them to me in your words, your actions certainly revealed them to me. Thank you for the kindness to those around you. Thank you for demonstrating generosity to the poor, the widows, and those who are just down on their luck in front of me. Thank you for your faith in Jesus that now lives within me and the realization that He desires for us to live in His abundance. Thank you for your stewardship over little and the faithfulness in the small so I could watch God bless it to grow into much. Finally, thank you for the risks that you have taken in your personal, professional, and spiritual lives. You've modeled all these principles by your life-both in my formative years and even continue to do so now. It is an honor to be your son.

To my wife, Kate. You have helped me articulate the lessons and concepts my parents taught me. You help draw out of me things I didn't even know that I contain and I'm eternally grateful for your love and support.

To my four sons, Maverick, Blaze, Phoenix, and Zephaniah. I pray the lessons in this book that opened doors of opportunity for your grandparents, your mother and me, and others practicing them are not only modeled in front of you, but also taught to you so that you may walk in all of the blessing that the LORD, has for you.

Table of Contents

Chapter 1 The Matthew Effect   1

Chapter 2 Giving   15

Chapter 3 Gratitude and Thankfulness   29

Chapter 4 Change the Way You Think   39

Chapter 5 Change the Way You Hear   53

Chapter 6 Faith   65

Chapter 7 Stewardship   77

Chapter 8 Goals and Declarations   87

Chapter 9 Activating the Matthew
          Effect in Your Life   97

Foreword

As a student of life and numerous subjects of interest, I find that books and their authors are inextricably linked together. Essentially, the author and his/her message are one and the same to me; therefore, when I choose to read, I open my mind and heart, not only to the subject matter, but especially to the perspective and influence of the author. If you are like me in recognizing that reading requires a measure of openness, even vulnerability on our part, I assure you that we are in good hands with Mark Wilburn and his excellent book, *The Matthew Effect!* The author and his subject matter are well-matched and thus powerfully impactful.

Mark is remarkable in so many areas of his life—as husband to Kate, co-parent to their four boys, son to his parents, friend to many of us privileged as such, and more. *The Matthew Effect* reflects Mark's outstanding revelation, understanding, and teaching ability in the area of finance, particularly wealth building. From my vantage point, the subject of wealth building, as part of the broader realm of Kingdom Finance, calls for the obtaining, retaining, and multiplication of financial resources. Mark's household and businesses have borne fruit in all three areas—and he is a master in instructing others how to engage with the processes that procure such results.

The Matthew Effect is a must-read for all of us who endeavor to co-labor with our Heavenly Father for the fulfillment of the covenant He made with Abraham, a solemn promise that, through Christ, we can access as part of our inheritance in Him. The must-read book comes from a must-engage-with Son, Mark Wilburn, who is hereby serving the Lord and our generations with exceptional riches of expertise and wisdom, built upon a solid foundation of godly character and integrity. It does not get better than this!

I wholeheartedly salute the author and his remarkable contribution to humanity, and I greet with honor and much love all of you who join us on this amazing journey!

Marios Ellinas
International Consultant &
Best-Selling Author
Connecticut, USA

Acknowledgments

Books are seldom, if ever, written as a solo project, and this book is no different. I would like to extend a great thanks to my publisher, Marti Statler, for her time and patience through this project; to Dennis McIntee whose great encouragement is what not only started but also continued to actually make this project happen. A massive thanks goes out to Steve Nance who helped make sense of so much of the content within this book using his master communication skills. Thank you to Nicole Kaspersen for her tremendous editing skills and insight, which make this book even better. Thank you also to Nicole Anonsen for her vision and graphic design skills, which transformed these concepts into graphic form. Thank you to my amazing family and friends for believing in me, and finally to the mentors in my life, both past and present, who have taught me, encouraged me, believed in me, and deposited themselves in me. Without each of you, I would not be the husband, father, and man that I am today. Thank you for your words, gifts, and trades into my life.

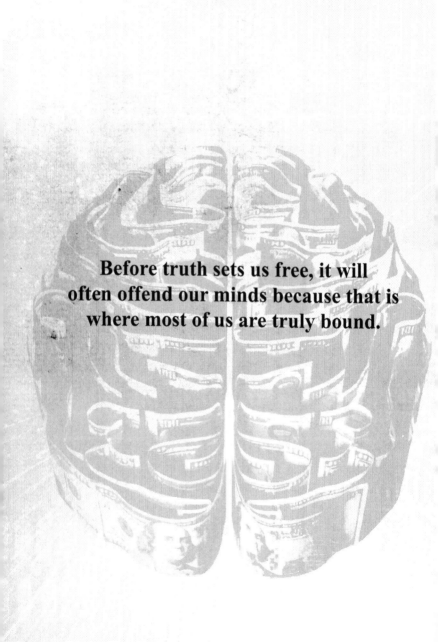

Before truth sets us free, it will
often offend our minds because that is
where most of us are truly bound.

Chapter One

The Matthew Effect

How often have you heard someone complain, "The rich get richer while the poor get poorer"? Maybe you've said it yourself. It's certainly not a new complaint, and it seems as though we're hearing it more and more these days, especially from the mouths of those who are often called "social justice warriors." Regardless of who says it, we almost always assume that it states a reality that is both negative and unjust. And while that may be true in many ways because of flawed human nature, the "mantra" that "the rich get richer while the poor get poorer" also states a principle that is built into the very structure of human life and experience. And while this principle is not exclusively spiritual, there's a massive spiritual element to it, just like anything else that God created. At heart, it is actually a business or economic principle called the Pareto Distribution. I would like to propose that this adage is a universal law that you can learn to tap into and use for your own benefit.

Although I've been engaging in this principle unknowingly for over a decade, the Lord in recent months has given me language for this that has really opened up a new revelation for me. It's an exciting revelation that I want to share with you because it can change your life like it has mine, not only in your business and economic pursuits, but also in virtually every other area of your life. I'm convinced that nothing the Lord does is limited to a single genre or arena of life. Anything that is truly of God is axiomatic and impacts every area of our lives. Whether our finances, our interpersonal relationships, our education, our attitude toward and understanding of media, or anything else we could think of, any true principle of heaven will have carryover impact in every area of life.

While the Pareto Distribution is not found in the Bible per se, it is very biblical in principle and operation. It is based on a social phenomenon that sociologist Robert Merton discovered in the 1970s and named "The Matthew Effect." Merton observed that in human society, accolades most often went to people of greater fame or notoriety, rather than to people less well-known, even if both did the very same thing. For example, in scientific research, senior scientists or researchers on a project receive the credit for new discoveries or breakthroughs even if those discoveries and breakthroughs were actually made by junior scientists or researchers, or even graduate students. Regardless of who does the actual work, the ones in charge get the credit.

In fact, The Matthew Effect itself is an example of this. Although Robert Merton discovered the Matthew Effect, he didn't receive initial credit for it. That accolade went to a man named Stephen Steigler, who created a "law" based on Merton's discovery, and which became known as "Steigler's Law of Autonomy." He even received an award for it. Even though Merton did the original work—which Steigler acknowledged at his award ceremony—Steigler received the credit because he was more well-known than Merton.

The Matthew Effect (and the related Pareto Distribution) literally is a mathematical "formula" that reveals one of God's laws in the earth. But hear me clearly: we must not confuse this with the Pareto *Principle*, also known as the 80/20 law, which says that 20 percent of the people in any business or organization do 80 percent of the work. I think we're all familiar with that principle. But if that sounds bad, the Pareto Distribution is even worse. It says that 50 percent of the work is done by the square root of the number of employees or the number of people in a given area. Hang with me here! Consider a company with one hundred employees. According to the 80/20 law, twenty employees do 80 percent of the work. But the Pareto Distribution says that ten employees (the square root of 100) in that company do 50 percent of the work. When you overlap these two principles, the math is astonishing: Out of the one hundred employees, twenty people (or 20 percent) are doing 80 percent of the work. Additionally, of those twenty people, ten people (the square root of the number of employees) are doing 50 percent (of the 80 percent) of that work. That means that there are there are eighty employees who aren't really doing much of anything at all.

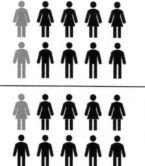

According to the Pareto Principle, 80% of the work is done by only 20% of the people

According to the Pareto Distribution, 50% of the work is done by the square root of the number of employees or in this case, 10% of the people

 = 10 employees

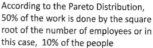

The fascinating thing about this distribution principle is that it applies in many areas of life, including population distribution and, of most interest to us in this book, wealth distribution. Let's look at a little data to get our heads around this. In the United States, the ten most populous states together have roughly the same population as the other forty states combined[1]. Considering the size and location of our major urban centers, that might sound reasonable. Breaking this down even further (and here's where it really gets nuts!), out of a total of 3,142 counties in the US, 145 together account for over 50.1 percent of the nation's population. This means that 49.9 percent of the population is distributed throughout the remaining 2,997 counties (many of which are referred to as "flyover country")[2].

[1] https://worldpopulationreview.com/states

[2] https://worldpopulationreview.com/us-counties

When it comes to wealth distribution, the data is even more startling. As of July 26, 2021, out of eight billion people in the world, there were 2,755 billion-aires[3]. And together, those 2,755 billionaires had more wealth than the bottom 4.6 billion people (over 50 per-cent) in the world. The combined wealth of the fifty richest Americans exceeds the combined wealth of the bottom 50 percent (165 million) of Americans[4]. Those kinds of numbers sound astronomical to us, and they are. They're staggering, almost inconceivable. And this takes us back to where I started: *The rich get richer, while the poor get poorer.* This is the principle that I want to teach you to begin leveraging in your life, today!

I grew up in your average middle-class family, and my parents worked extremely hard to give my sister and me the best "leg up" they could. My father was a schoolteacher and minister, and my mother was and still is an entrepreneur in the truest sense. They both worked hard, saved their money, modeled frugality in their finances in order to pay off their debt, and taught me more lessons by their actions than their words ever could. They never spoke ill of wealthier people; actu-ally, they never spoke ill of anyone. They were gen-erous givers to those less fortunate even though we

---

[3] https://www.forbes.com/sites/kerryadolan/2021/04/06/forbes-35th-annual-worlds-billionaires-list-facts-and-figures-2021/?sh=5fd76c4d5e58

[4] https://www.bloomberg.com/news/articles/2020-10-08/top-50-richest-people-in-the-us-are-worth-as-much-as-poorest-165-million

did not have a large abundance ourselves. They were (and still are) always quick to model gratitude to the Almighty for what He has given them.

As an adult, when I look back, I realize their wealth grew because they were able to engage the principles laid out in this book. One thing they

God brings opportunities in our lives that can change our financial future.

did teach me is that God brings opportunities in our lives that can change our financial future. However, I still heard that phrase, "the rich get richer" growing up. At first, I took it to be a slight against rich people. But as I grew older, I began to see it as a challenge or even an invitation: *if I could get rich, then I could get richer.* That's just the way my mind works. I thought that if I could tap into that, then I could start having it work for me.

But today we often hear people railing against "those stingy rich people" who are taking all this wealth and hoarding it. That's a word being thrown around a lot these days: *hoarding*. And it's not just the social justice warriors who are saying it; many of our political leaders are doing the same: "Such a disparity of wealth is unfair," they insist. "It's unjust. It's not right. They should give more of their money away or pay their 'fair share' in taxes!"

To be honest, I think all of this is evil and misguided talk. My proposal to you reading this book is that these wealthy individuals have tapped into something significant; they've tapped into a law that works on their behalf to help them accumulate more and more and more wealth, a law that is built into the very structure of the world and human relationships.

Wealthy individuals have tapped into something significant.

Deuteronomy 8:18 says, "But remember the LORD your God, for it is He who gives you the ability to produce wealth, and so confirms His covenant, which He swore to your ancestors, as it is today." Notice that it is God Himself who enables us to produce wealth. I see this as both an opportunity and a challenge. This is much more than just a statement that the rich get richer; it is an economic principle, a biblical and divine law that has been written into the earth. And this is where we see the significance of the name The *Matthew* Effect; when we research this in the Bible, we find it in five different places in the gospels.

The first occurrence is in the Matthew 13. Jesus has just finished telling His famous parable of the sower and the seed. His disciples come to Him with a question. "'Why do you speak to the people in parables?' He replied, 'Because the knowledge of the secrets of the kingdom of Heaven has been given to you, but not to them.'" (Matt. 13:10b-11). Time out. Hold on a minute. Is he really saying that the twelve disciples (or seventy or one hundred twenty; we really don't know exactly how many) have the ability to understand and explain the "secrets of the kingdom of Heaven"? Why did Jesus grant that ability to this particular group but not to the others? Does that seem fair to you? What we see here is the Pareto Distribution in action. Let's keep reading. Jesus continued, "Whoever has will be given more, and they will have an abundance. Whoever does not have, even what they have will be taken from them" (Matt. 13:12). Does that really mean what it sounds like it means? Is he really saying that the "haves" will be given more while the "have nots" will lose the little they have? We hear this and it violates our sense of societal justice. We want everybody to be "equal." We want everybody to play on the same level playing field. We want to lift everybody up. How is it fair to take away the little that someone has and give it to someone who already has an abundance? That doesn't make sense. That's the view of the "social justice" world, and while it sounds reasonable and logical and even compassionate, it is not biblical. It is not a spiritual truth. The current call for "wealth redistribution" programs that would take money from the rich whether they like it or not and give it to the poor, all in the name of "justice," "equity," and a "level playing field," is not just anti-Christian it's actually anti-Bible. It is contrary to what Jesus taught. I understand that might bother some of you, but I'm merely pointing out what the Bible says about this matter. It's up to you to come to terms with it. That's what Jesus said, and I believe it is the truth. John 8:32 says, "You will know the truth, and the truth will set you free." However, before truth sets us free, it often offends our mind because that is where most of us are truly bound.

He reiterates the same principle in another parable, the parable of the talents in Matthew 25. In this story, a wealthy man, before leaving on a journey, entrusts some of his wealth to three of his servants. He gives five "talents" ("bags of gold" NIV) to one servant, two talents to another, and one talent to the third. While the first two servants double their money through wise trading (and business), the third servant simply hides his talent and does nothing. Upon his return, their master calls them to account, and while he praises the first two for their wise stewardship, he punishes the third servant who didn't even try to use what he had. In the climax to the parable, the master says, "So take the bag of gold from him and give it to the one who has ten bags. For whoever has will be given more, and they will have an abundance. Whoever does not have, even what they have will be taken from them" (Matt. 25:28-29).

So, twice in the Gospel of Matthew we have Jesus saying the exact same thing; hence, the Matthew Effect: the rich get richer. The question is why. Why do those with much gain more, and why do those with little lose what little they have? To answer that, we need to look at the other three examples in the gospels where Jesus speaks to this.

Luke 8:16-18 records a shorter parable about a lamp. Jesus says that no one lights a lamp and then hides it in a clay jar or under the bed but sets it on a lampstand so that everyone can see the light. He then declares that there is nothing concealed that will not be brought to light. His closing words should, by now, be very familiar. "Therefore consider carefully how you listen. Whoever has will be given more; whoever does not have, even what they think they have will be taken from them" (Luke 8:18).

Looking further into Luke, we come to Jesus' parable of the minas, one of my favorite parables when it comes to money. A man of noble birth, before leaving on a journey to be appointed king, calls ten of his servants and gives them ten minas (a mina was about 3 months' wages) and tells them to "*Put this money to work...*until I come back" (emphasis added). Upon his return he calls his servants to account, but Luke only records three of them. The first servant, who has earned ten minas from his original one, is rewarded by being placed in charge of ten cities. Likewise, the second servant, who has earned five minas, is given five cities. The third servant, however, who has done nothing with his master's mina except bury it, has it taken away from him and given to the servant who has ten minas. This action puzzles those standing around him. "'Sir,' they said, 'he already has ten!' He replied, 'I tell you that to everyone who has, more will be given, but as for the one who has nothing, even what they have will be taken away'" (Luke 19:25-26).

The only person who got in trouble was the guy who literally did nothing with what he had. Instead of using it, he buried it. We've got to remember that these are parables dealing with business. If I'm giving out money to "put it to work," do I want to give it to a person who's going to bury it, or to a person who's going to use it wisely and give me a return? Obviously, the person who will bring me the bigger return. Trust is a foundational element that fuels the operation of the Matthew Effect.

> **Trust is a foundational element that fuels the operation of the Matthew Effect.**

Our final scriptural example is found in Mark chapter four. As in Luke, this is Jesus's parable of the sower, followed by the parable of the lamp on a stand. The conclusion of that second parable in Mark's version is a little different from Luke's. Jesus says, "If anyone has ears to hear, let them hear. Consider carefully what you hear...With the measure you use, it will be measured to you—and even more. Whoever has will be given more; whoever does not have, even what they have will be taken from them" (Mark 4:23-25).

And so, again, we hear this as "the rich get richer, while the poor get poorer." However, I have come to realize that this is a law in the universe. Whenever I hear people say, "The stock market only benefits the rich," I think to myself, "Okay, if the rich are getting richer off the stock market, I need to engage the stock market." If rich people are getting richer in the real estate market, I need to engage the real estate market. If people complain, "Buying gold and silver only helps people who have it," then I need to be buying gold and silver.

So, what are some things we can do to put ourselves in the position where this law works for us? First, we need to understand and take hold of the truth that Jesus is so good to us, that He would not give us these principles without giving us the ability to insert ourselves into them and benefit from them. I believe it's His heart for us to put ourselves in a position where we can begin to compound riches and wealth in our own life and begin a domino-effect process of wealth building that will carry across the years of our lives and flow over into succeeding generations, so that we and our descendants are the ones who are rich and getting richer.

There is a powerful chapter in Genesis chapter 18, when three supernatural beings, on their way to destroy Sodom and Gomorrah, stop for a meal at Abraham's tent. The Bible identifies one of these three as the Lord. As they leave, Abraham walks with them for a short distance. "Then the LORD said, 'Shall I hide from Abraham what I am about to do? Abraham will surely become a great and powerful nation, and all nations on earth will be blessed through him. For I have chosen him, so that he will direct his children and his household after him to keep the way of the LORD by doing what is right and just, so that the LORD will bring about for Abraham what he has promised him'" (Gen. 18:17-19). I believe that GOD is so good—that Jesus is so good—that He has shown us this principle. All we need are eyes to see it. Throughout His word He has given keys to unlock our ability to step into a position so that this principle, the Matthew Effect, starts working on our behalf. If I had to describe the purpose of this book and the teachings behind it, I would call it "Hacking the Pareto Distribution," just like a computer hacker who breaks into something that seems locked to everyone else, so you will learn to tap into this powerful principle as well. In the chapters that follow, I will discuss six critical keys for "unlocking" the Matthew Effect so you can benefit from it, as well as some practical tips for identifying, declaring, and energizing your goals to help make this work for you.

Welcome to the adventure!

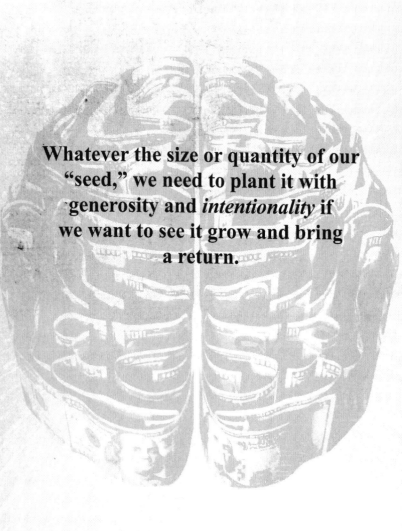

Whatever the size or quantity of our
"seed," we need to plant it with
generosity and *intentionality* if
we want to see it grow and bring
a return.

Chapter Two

Giving

Giving? Really? If we're talking about hacking the Pareto Distribution and building wealth, why start with giving? Where's the logic in that? I know it might seem counterintuitive but remember that we are dealing with a spiritual principle, a universal law built into the very fabric of creation by God. Therefore, we should remember that His thoughts and His ways are higher than ours (Isa. 55:8-9), so it shouldn't surprise us that the keys for unlocking this principle would be different than we might expect. This being the case, I believe with all my heart that one of the first ways to get into this principle is by giving and trading. When I say giving, I mean giving your time and money to charities, ministries, to the poor and needy, etc., which we'll look at shortly. When I talk about trading, I am not only speaking about investing in stocks (which I would highly encourage you to both learn and do), but also much more: I believe that everything we do, every action we take, is a type of "trade." People trade their time for money at a job. I can trade an opportunity to exercise for a chance to play with my children. Here, however, I would like for you to think of trading as an extension of the law of "sowing and reaping" (Galatians 6:7). When a speaker attends a conference and you hear a word that may bring about increase in your everyday life, you can trade into (or give to) that speaker. This act places both a spiritual and financial expectation on those words. You receive the words (sowing) and they will help you grow, mature, and bear fruit (reaping). You are, in essence, trading a commodity for the words you hear. In doing so, you can now activate those words and apply them to your life.

Proverbs 11:24 states concisely the counterintuitive nature of this principle: "One person gives freely, yet gains even more; another withholds unduly, but comes to poverty." One person "gives freely" (think of sowing or scattering seed) and receives increase, while another hoards what he has, only to see it dwindle away. That doesn't make logical sense, does it? Human logic tells us that we must hang onto what little we have; we can't afford to give; we can't run the risk of trading in the hope of getting something better. But we're only fooling ourselves. *We all have something we can give.*

Observing the principle of giving is more important than the *level (or financial amount)* of giving. Start giving what you can from where you are. If you can't trade with $100 bills, trade with tens. If you can't with tens, do it with fives or ones. If pennies are all you have to start with, don't let that stop you. Give anyway from a generous spirit and watch for an increase. One day in Jerusalem, Jesus and His disciples watched as rich people dropped bags of money into the temple treasury. Then a widow came up and dropped in a "mite," two copper coins worth only a few cents. Observing this, Jesus said to His disciples, "Truly I tell you, this poor widow has put more into the treasury than all the others. They all gave out of their wealth; but she, out of her poverty, put in everything—all she had to live on" (Mk. 12:43b-44). She gave to God and trusted in His increase—to care for her.

Giving not only opens a realm of increase but IS a realm of increase that we can all step into. The more generously we give, or scatter our seed, the greater will be our

> **Giving not only opens a realm of increase but IS a realm of increase that we can all step into.**

increase: "Give, and it will be given to you. A good measure, pressed down, shaken together and running over, will be poured into your lap. For with the measure you use, it will be measured to you" (Lk. 6:38). One reason we so easily get hung up about giving is that we don't measure what we're giving; we don't evaluate the cost of what we might give against the return, or benefit, we would derive from our giving. Whatever the size or quantity of our "seed," we need to plant it with generosity and *intentionality* if we want to see it grow and bring a return. Generosity means giving sincerely from our heart, while intentionality has to do with our personal desire attached to our giving—what we want to see manifest in our lives that will lift us higher.

Three "Trading Floors" for Giving

There are many different ways to give, regardless of whether we're giving money, time, or energy. One way to look at this is to think of levels or "trading floors" of giving, as when dealing with stocks. I could trade Apple stock by purchasing the shares for a potential return of, let's say, 5 percent. However, I could sell an option for a potential return of 15 percent, or I could buy an option for a potential return of 35 percent plus. The different ways we give, I believe, determine the potential of the return we are likely to receive. In the remainder of this chapter, I want to focus on three particular "trading floors" that are critical to this first key for unlocking the Matthew Effect—the key of giving. These three floors are tithing, giving to the poor, and giving to widows and orphans.

Tithing

Tithing is an ancient concept that is not strictly a "religious" practice. It is often paired with another level of giving, as in "tithes and offerings." Although the word "tithe" literally means "10 percent," the practice of tithing involves setting aside or giving a specific amount or percentage of our assets to a specific cause or group. For example, we could give to a 501(c) nonprofit that does cancer research, a religious group that feeds the hungry, or a humanitarian organization that provides free medical care. From the perspective of a Christian worldview, the tithe is thought of as going into the "storehouse" of the church. From a Jewish perspective, it might be giving to your local community, whether cancer research, a school project you're passionate about, support of your local church and its ministries, giving to help the poor and other needy persons in the community. In the local church, the tithe of 10 percent of one's income is regarded as customary as a basic starting place. "Offerings" then refers to any gifts above and beyond the basic tithe. Having said that, for some of you reading this, giving 10 percent of your income could scare you. That's okay! I would challenge you to start with something smaller and work your way up because this is an extremely important concept.

How important is this principle of tithes and offerings? Scripture associates it with the difference between being blessed or cursed: In Malachi 3, God asks the prophet: "'Will a man rob God? Yet you rob me. But you ask, "How are we robbing you?" In tithes and offerings. You are under a curse—your whole nation—because you are robbing me. Bring the whole tithe into the storehouse, that there may be food in my house. Test me in this, says the LORD Almighty, 'and see if I will not throw open the floodgates of heaven and pour out so much blessing that there will not be room enough to store it'" (Mal. 3:8-10).

This is one of the only places in scripture where God actually invites us—even challenges us—to test Him, to test His faithfulness. So, when we give tithes and offerings (notice that it's not one or the other, but both), and do it from a generous heart, He opens a door to have His blessing on our lives. I know there are many Christians who say that we don't have to tithe because we are under the new covenant, but the principle of the tithe predates the covenant, whether old or new. If you want to unlock the Matthew Effect—if you want to hack the Pareto Distribution—let the tithe and other offerings be your baseline. If you want to walk into abundance, let tithes and offerings be your starting place.

What is the benefit of tithing though? "'And I will rebuke the devourer for your sakes, So that he will not destroy the fruit of your ground, Nor shall the vine fail to bear fruit for you in the field,' Says the LORD of hosts; 'And all nations will call you blessed, For you will be a delightful land,' Says the LORD of hosts" (Mal. 3:11-12 NKJV).

Giving to the Poor

If trading floor number one is giving tithes and offerings, trading floor number two is giving to the poor. This is a particularly powerful way to both help other people and put yourself in the Pareto Distribution. This one is my favorite, not only because it's fun and gratifying to help people in need, but also because it comes with some mind-blowing scriptural promises. Listen to this: "Whoever is kind to the poor lends to the LORD, and he will reward them for what they have done" (Prov. 19:17). If we *lend* to the LORD when we are kind to the poor, that means He places Himself in the position of a *borrower* from us. I'll get back to that in a minute, let's add another scripture to that one. "The rich rule over the poor, and the borrower is slave to the lender" (Prov. 22:7). Many people take this verse to mean that we should never need to borrow money or go into debt. While that certainly is a form of wise counsel and a worthy goal, it is not universal. This mindset of "not having any debt" is a massive illusion that keeps many people from reaching the financial freedom they desire. Not all borrowing or debt is bad. In fact, debt can be a great tool to help us grow wealth if we understand how to leverage it properly. However, that is a conversation for another time. The point of the scripture is that if "the borrower is slave to the lender," we need to be very careful who we borrow from and why we are borrowing.

Now, let's put these two verses together and see what we've got. If we are kind to the poor, we *lend* to God, and the borrower is *slave* to the lender. Do you see where I'm going with this? If we lend to God when we are kind to the poor, God becomes our borrower. This means that He puts Himself in the position of our slave, so to speak, to repay us. When we give to the poor, God, by His own words, indebts Himself to pay us back. In effect, He signs a promissory note to reimburse us—with interest (blessings). The latter part of Proverbs 19:17 guarantees it: "[the LORD] will reward them for what they have done." This is His promise, and He always keeps His promises.

> **When we give to the poor, God, by His own words, indebts Himself to pay us back.**

This is a massive principle for opening our lives to blessings, which is one reason why Jesus said, "It is more blessed to give than to receive" (Acts 20:35b). When we receive a gift, it has static value; it may be nice, or even expensive or valuable, but it has no capacity to grow. When we give, however, especially to those who cannot pay us back, we receive back from the hand of God what we gave, but with multiplied value added. The poor we're talking about are not only the destitute, the homeless, the hungry—anyone in need who cannot meet those needs themselves, but people who do not have the ability to repay us. When we give directly to those kind of people, we are lending to God, and He will pay that debt—and much more.

Giving to the poor doesn't always mean giving them money—not directly, at least. That's a hang up many of us have. We see a guy on the street holding a sign saying "Hungry, please help," or "Jobless, need money," and we may want to help, but—and we've all thought this—we suspect that if we give him some money, he will just use it for drugs or alcohol, so we do nothing. There's actually a stigma around that. Jewish culture, however, teaches us that what he does with the money is not our responsibility. Our responsibility is simply to give.

But let's say we wanted to help him in ways other than giving him money directly. What could we do? I used to live in Sarasota, Florida, which had a large homeless population. A buddy of mine, who at one time had been homeless himself, told me that some of

the things he always wanted were a clean pair of under-
wear, or a clean pair of socks, and other practical things
like toothpaste, shampoo, and soap. He and I started
putting together gift bags containing those items,
which we handed out to homeless people we met. How
much money do you invest in providing those items?
A few bucks. But it's a great way to get started in this
powerful principle of giving to the poor.

Another thing I like to do is carry around with me
at least three or four packs of crackers, protein bars,
some type of snack and some bottles of water in my
car, so I can hand them out when someone on the street
tells me they're hungry or thirsty. It's a small thing, but
sometimes it's the small things that make all the difference. And small things are what any one of us can do,
regardless of our particular circumstances.

Another great way to give to the poor is to buy
canned and other non-perishable foods and donate
them to a local food pantry. That way you can be more
confident that what you give actually gets into the
hands of the poor. You can also give money directly to
the food pantry so they can shop for items they need
for helping people. The secret is to target those oper-
ations where your giving will have the most direct
impact on the lives of the poor.

You can do the same thing with used clothing or
furniture that you're replacing. Goodwill Industries is
one good option, but they will turn around and sell your
donations, though at a very low price that most can
afford. Rather than going to Goodwill, however, you
might consider asking your pastor if there is a family in

need of these particular goods. You can look for a local clothing pantry to donate your gently used clothing to as well. Along with community-sponsored services, many churches and religious organizations operate food and clothing pantries. These are great ways to make many of the everyday necessities of life available for free to those who cannot afford to buy them.

Scripture clearly teaches that God has a special place in His heart for the poor. When you give to the poor, you lend to God, and He, as the borrower, will repay you. And one of the most satisfying rewards of this is the joy that comes with helping others simply because you can.

Giving to Widows and Orphans

Widows and orphans may sometimes be a subset of the poor, but they constitute a separate, third "trading floor" for giving because the New Testament book of James clearly separates them from the poor and tells us that "Religion that God our Father accepts as pure and faultless is this: to look after orphans and widows in their distress and to keep oneself from being polluted by the world" (Jas. 1:27). Because many widows and orphans are poor, at least in the sense of having no close relations to help them in their need, the reward for giving to these needy ones is similar for giving to the poor in general. However, this goes one step beyond the promise that if we give to the poor, God, Himself, repays us, as widows and orphans hold a special place in His heart. In all honesty, this is a mystery I am still unfolding, but I have experienced exponential blessings firsthand and would be remiss not to disclose it to you. God blesses those who bless the poor, the widows, and the orphans, especially when they do so in His name. This doesn't mean that you are kind to tell them, "The LORD bless you"; it means the intention of your heart is to bless them as if blessing the LORD. This could be anybody: a woman in your church who needs a conversation partner, a child in your neighborhood who needs a mentor, or someone who needs help with "handyman" projects such as cutting grass, cleaning gutters, or doing small repairs. This could look like providing transportation for doctor appointments or grocery shopping which may fill a vital need in someone's life. Also, for those who are in a position to do it, foster parenting or adoption are both great ways to care for orphans. There are numerous ways to help widows & orphans in our community and abroad if we begin to think outside the box and, I can promise, The LORD is eager to pour out blessing on those who step-up.

There is great benefit to giving to the poor and helping widows and orphans. And giving doesn't always have to be monetary. Many times, giving of our time, attention, and compassion is the most valuable of all. So, there are many things we can do to put ourselves in that giving position. But putting money where finances are sorely needed is extremely powerful because we reap what we sow. When we sow money, we reap money.

> **Giving of our time, attention, and compassion is the most valuable of all.**

If you are looking for a place to donate money that will go directly to help widows and orphans, I have an amazing friend in South Africa who is a widow herself and also helps support numerous orphanages around the continent of Africa. You can find her and donate to her and her cause at: https://www.ignitehubs.org/

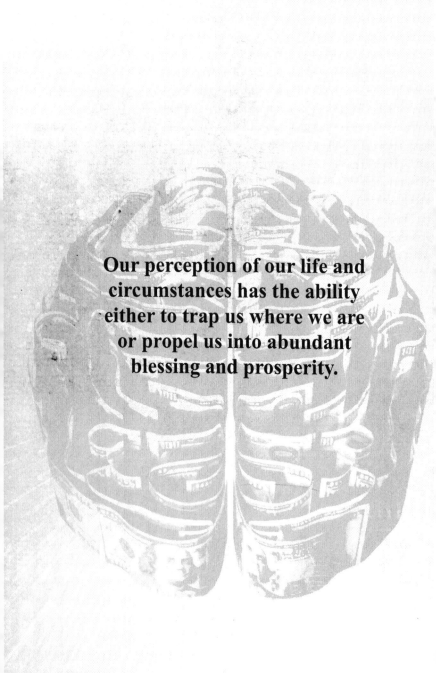

Our perception of our life and circumstances has the ability either to trap us where we are or propel us into abundant blessing and prosperity.

Chapter Three

Gratitude and Thankfulness

We have just seen how giving—having a generous heart—is the first critical key for hacking the Pareto Distribution. The second key, closely related to the first, also involves a "heart condition": having a grateful heart, a habitual attitude of gratitude and thankfulness. This means learning to be grateful *now* for your life and circumstances as they currently are, and being thankful for what you have *right now*, rather than just dreaming of what you hope to have one day.

My wife and I own a stock trading education company called NEOS Capital Development Group. Whenever new clients come in, I listen carefully to the way they talk about their money, because most people, *unknowingly*, curse their money before they even get started. Many of them come in assuming they need ten thousand dollars, twenty-five thousand dollars, or even fifty thousand dollars to get started. Then they often say something like, "I only have five hundred dollars to work with, and what is that?" I used to tell clients that they could start with "as little as" five hundred dollars (or whatever amount). But the Lord showed me that I needed to change the way I spoke, so now I'll say, "You can start with five hundred dollars." Do you see the difference? To say "I *only* have"...or "you can start with *as little as*" speaks from a position or attitude of *lack*, both of assets and expectations. But to say, "Start with what you have" is different, because it places no pre-assumed limits on where you can go once you do start.

This brings to mind the New Testament account of Jesus feeding more than five thousand people with some fish and a few loaves of bread. This account appears in all four Gospels, but I'll illustrate with John's account. Surrounded by a very large crowd who had come to hear for teaching and healing, He knew they were hungry and He wanted to feed them. Testing His disciples (because He already knew what He was going to do), Jesus asked them where they could buy enough bread to feed the people. One of them replied that not even half a year's wages would be enough, while another, Andrew, surveyed their assets and asked a very natural question: "Here is a boy with five small barley loaves and two small fish, but how far will they go among so many?" (Jn. 6:9). That is the same thing that so many people do with their own finances. I only have five hundred dollars to start trading, how far will that go in creating my financial future? "How far will they go" is another way of saying, "we only have..." Limited thinking, limited vision, limited return.

If we start off focusing on what we don't have, we're only cursing our seed before we even plant it in the ground. Suppose I showed you an apple seed and asked you, "What is this?" Some of you might say, "That's an apple seed," and you would be right. Others might say, "That's an apple tree," and you also would be right. Still other people might say, "That's an apple orchard," which is also correct. The difference is vision. Do you see only short-range, the immediate right in front of you, or can you see long-range, generationally down the pipeline? One seed becomes a tree, which produces many seeds, which produce many more trees with many more seeds, until you have not one apple tree that can feed a few, but an entire grove that can feed a multitude. It all depends on how far we can see. Jesus did not focus on the limited reality before Him, but on the unlimited potentiality He was about to draw upon. After the people were seated (five thousand men plus women and children), Jesus did a very important thing: "[He] then took the loaves, gave thanks, and distributed to those who were seated as much as they wanted. He did the same with the fish" (Jn. 6:11, emphasis added). Do you see what He did? Jesus gave thanks for the provision even before it occurred. Deliberate thanks from a grateful heart was the key that unlocked abundance that fed a multitude: everyone was fed, and there were twelve basketfuls of leftovers.

Our perception of our life and circumstances has the ability either to trap us where we are or propel us into abundant blessing and prosperity. And how does that start? With sincere gratitude and thankfulness, regardless of current circumstances. Think about these words from James, the brother of Jesus: "Consider it pure joy, my brothers and sisters, whenever you face trials of many kinds, because you know that the testing of your faith produces perseverance. Let perseverance finish its work so that you may be mature and complete, not lacking anything" (Jas. 1:2-4, emphasis added). "Pure joy" and gratitude go together, and while "not lacking anything" refers to more than just money, it certainly includes money. So, if we're not lacking anything, that means, among other things, that we have money. We have abundance. We have provision in every area of life. In the story of Jesus feeding the 5000, the difference between Andrew and Jesus was that Andrew saw limitations—"how far will they go among so many?"—while Jesus saw the same thing but looked beyond it and gave thanks for what He had, knowing that He was lifting this into the kingdom dimension of His Father's unlimited supply, from which He could multiply and distribute it here to meet everyone's needs. What made the difference was gratitude and thankfulness. So, instead of saying, "All I've got is five hundred dollars," say, "Thank God, I have five hundred dollars I can start with!" It's a totally different mindset, a complete paradigm shift, but it makes all the difference in the world. And it all has to do with gratitude and thankfulness in our hearts. Couple this with the long-term vision, and five hundred dollars could grow into the fifty thousand dollars that most people think they need to begin with!

Scripture commands us to give thanks in all things: "Make sure that nobody pays back wrong for wrong, but always strive to do what is good for each other and for everyone else. Rejoice always, pray continually, give thanks in all circumstances; for this is God's will for you in Christ Jesus" (1 Thess. 5:16-18, emphasis added). And in another place: "always giving thanks to God the Father for everything, in the name of

> **In an atmosphere of gratitude—and only in such an atmosphere—change and increase are possible.**

our Lord Jesus Christ" (Eph. 5:20, emphasis added). In these and other places the apostle Paul commands us to be thankful. Why? Because he knew that in an atmosphere of gratitude—and only in such an atmosphere—change and increase are possible.

If you express thanks for something someone does for you, it causes that person to want to do it again. If I bring my wife flowers and she thanks me for them, it makes me want to repeat the gift. But suppose I bring her flowers and she rejects the gift: "What? Lilies again! You know I prefer roses!" I'm not likely to bring her any more flowers in the near future. Why? Because it hurts to have her despise my gift. Zechariah 4:10 says, "Do not despise these small beginnings, for the Lord rejoices to see the work begin..." (NLT). Don't despise what you have just because it seems small to you. A seed is a small beginning, but one that can grow into a tree that bears abundant fruit. That fruit will produce more seeds, which will grow into more trees. Those trees will turn into groves and forests of abundance that will feed everything around you. To whomever has, more will be given.

If I have a seed (money, an idea, etc.), what am I going to do? I'm going to plant that seed and nurture it into a tree. I'm going to nurture this business market. Maybe I've only got a small idea, the idea, say, of selling used college textbooks on the internet. Sound silly? Too small to bother with? Jeff Bezos didn't think so. He didn't despise his idea. He thought it would work, so he planted it, nurtured it, and watched it grow into Amazon, one of the largest retailers in the world.

Don't despise your small ideas or small assets. Plant them and nurture them; you never know how they could grow and grow until they develop massive momentum.

> **Don't despise your small ideas or small assets. Plant them and nurture them.**

This is why it's so important to bless the infancy of a thing. Bless the infancy of your business. Bless the infancy of your finances. Maybe you just paid off one credit card but have four more weighing you down with large balances. Rather than getting down and out over those four, bless the fact that one is out of the way. Be grateful and give thanks: "Thank you, Father, that I've been able to pay off that credit card." "Thank you, Father, that I got that raise." Once you begin to operate from a place of heartfelt gratitude and thankfulness, the whole atmosphere around you will shift, and you will begin to attract more. Being vocal in our thanks for the things we have attracts more of it to us. Gratitude, like giving, is a universal spiritual principle for abundance in all of life, including money and finances.

Someone once said, "Watch your words because your words create your worlds." That is so true. Scripture even says, "With the fruit of a person's mouth his stomach will be satisfied; He will be satisfied *with* the product of his lips. Death and life are in the power of the tongue, and those who love it will eat its fruit." (Prov 18:20-21). Many people know and even quote the first part of verse 21, but most don't finish it. "Those who love it will eat its fruit." If we speak blessing, we will eat of those blessings, but if we speak curses, we will eat of those curses. What kind of world, what kind of fruit, do you want to create for yourself? I pray it's one of blessing and abundance!

There is no way a person can be negative and thankful at the same time. I heard a story a while back about a husband and wife who got into a huge argument. The room was full of anger and hurt. The husband walked outside and began to talk to God about it. He complained to God left and right about his wife. Finally God said, *"Okay, now tell me something good about your wife."*

The husband was so angry that, at first, he couldn't think of anything. *"Nothing. There's nothing good about that woman,"* he insisted.

The Lord kept prompting him. *"Just one good thing."*

The husband thought for a little bit and then conceded, *"Well, she's a good mother."*

"What makes her a good mother?" the Lord asked.

"The way she takes care of the kids. She makes their lunches for school every day. She treats their cuts and bruises and comforts them when they're scared." As he began thinking of the little things that were good about his wife, other good things about her came to mind. *"She's a good cook and is faithful about preparing our meals."* He went on for twenty minutes thinking about and expressing good things. about his wife, and went back in the house thinking, *"I've got the best wife in the world!"*

I'm sure many of us can identify with that story. The point is that whenever we're upset with a situation, if we can turn it around and find the good in that thing, it actually blocks the negativity and the bad stuff from really impacting us. Sometimes that's hard to do, especially during a major crisis, such as losing a loved one. Look for the good in any situation. Maybe you have a bad day at work. Ask yourself, "What was a highlight for me at work today? What was something good that happened?" Most likely, you'll discover that your whole day wasn't a disaster. It's human nature to dwell on the negative, so we have to be proactive in learning to look for the positive.

Before we end this chapter, I want to give you a small exercise that I learned from one of my mentors. This simple step has made a huge difference in my mindsets on how I end and approach each day. I call this, finding your "win" for the day. Here's how it works at the end of each day when my family and I are sitting down for dinner, we ask each person, what was your "win" for the day? Once the person shares, we celebrate those together as a family. What is a win? A win can be as simple as taking five minutes to meditate or read. A win is something that you did or happened that brought joy/happiness to your life and what's great is YOU get to define it!

This exercise allows each person to find and focus on something good that has happened to them in their day, rather than allow those "bad" moments to hijack the day. Personally, I like repeating those same wins (from the previous day) the next morning to myself which starts the next day from a place of victory rather than dread. It helps me walk into my day as a champion. Let me encourage you to always look for something good you can take away and focus on, because what we focus on, we attract. And when we focus on the positive, it is easier to approach life with gratitude and thankfulness, and we can start living and looking for those things to multiply in our lives. Being thankful for what we have attracts more of it to us. And not only that, we literally see the attraction manifest. That's what thankfulness does. And that's the power of an attitude of gratitude.

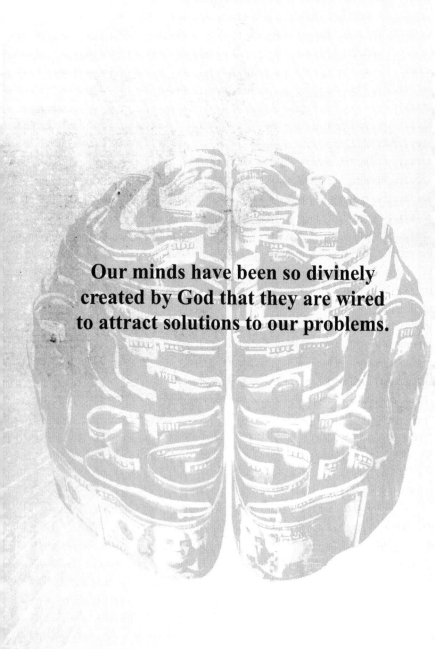

Our minds have been so divinely created by God that they are wired to attract solutions to our problems.

Chapter Four

Change the Way You Think

As we have seen, our first two keys for hacking the Pareto Distribution involve a "heart change":

> **The sky is not your limit—your mind is.**

giving generously from an attitude of sincere gratitude and thankfulness. The third critical key involves a "mind change": if we want to build wealth and see the Matthew Effect manifest in our lives, we have to change the way we *think*. About money. About people. About ourselves. About life in general. More people fail to realize their dreams because of mental barriers than probably any other single cause. I heard someone once say, "The sky is not your limit; your mind is." The way we think affects every aspect of our lives, and most of us are limited by our thinking in ways we don't even realize because our modes of thinking have been ingrained in us from our earliest years. I can promise you that wealthy people think differently than poor people. They think differently about risk, opportunity, how they make money, how they spend money, taxes, and what success even looks like. The good news is that if we change the way we think, then we can change the course of our lives.

Proverbs 23:7 says, "For as [a man] thinks in his heart, so is he" (NKJV). In other words, we become what we think and what we ponder. So, if we want to change who we are, or change our life circumstances, we must change the way we think. The apostle Paul, a pretty sharp thinker himself, said, "Do not conform to the pattern of this world, but be transformed by the renewing of your mind. Then you will be able to test and approve what God's will is—his good, pleasing and perfect will" (Rom. 12:2). So, this change or "renewing" of our mind goes right along with the first two keys of giving and gratitude; actually, they're inseparable. With that in mind, let me ask you: How do *you* think about money? About wealth? About rich people? What do *you* think about being an entrepreneur and owning your own business? What do *you* think about sales and retail? How do you *really* feel about "The rich get richer and the poor get poorer"? As for me, I'm one of those people who gets richer. You too can be one of those people who get richer, but you have to begin to change the way you think—not only from a conscious level, but from a subconscious level as well. Changing your mind is easy, it's changing your heart that is a bit more difficult. James says "...a double minded man is unstable in all his ways" (James1:8). How can we have two minds unless one is our conscious mind and one is in our subconscious or heart? We hear people say, "I know this doesn't make sense, but I know in my heart..." and almost always, the heart-mind is the correct mind. As we begin to change the way we think in our heart and our mind, we actually begin to attract those things to us. Napoleon Hill wrote an amazing book on finances called, *Think and Grow Rich*, that I highly recommend. If you are in business or want to go into business, you really need to read this book, because it contains some incredible and powerful spiritual principles for adopting the proper mental framework for building wealth.

> **Changing our mind is easy; it's changing our heart that is a bit more difficult.**

A change of mind (or thinking) is one meaning of the Greek word *metanoia*, or "repent" that we find in the New Testament. *Metanoia* is made up of *meta* (higher) and *noia* (thinking). So, literally, it means "thinking at a higher level." Albert Einstein famously said, "No problem can be solved from the same level of consciousness that created it." We have to think higher than that. Changing the way we think opens up the opportunity for us to personally engage the mentality that "the rich get richer," and thus hack the Pareto Distribution. Our minds are powerful problem solvers. As we learn to think habitually about these things, we begin to attract them to us.

To help illustrate this, think about what happens when you buy a new car. Once you start driving it, you start seeing others of the same model wherever you go. Suddenly, it seems as if everyone on the road is driving the same kind of car as you. Many years ago, when I was living in Florida and just starting to get into this stuff, I was doing some dream-boarding—writing down my dreams and desires and placing them as images on the board that I could look at and meditate on. One of my dreams at that time was to own a silver Jaguar XKR SuperSport. I even went down to the Jaguar dealership where I lived and took it for a test drive. It was kind of funny, because when I told the salesman I wanted to test drive it he gave me a strange look and said, "Oh, really? You really want to do this?"

I said, "Absolutely!" So, I jumped in and took it for a spin.

When I got back he asked, "Well, are you ready to sign the papers?"

"Not quite," I told him.

At that time all I really wanted was to get the feel of it, to experience what it was like to be behind the wheel of such an awesome car. But then I noticed that I started seeing this car everywhere I went, that same Jaguar XKR Supersport. Why? Because I had it so ingrained in my subconscious that my mind started finding solutions to the problem. When we become wealth oriented, and when we become business oriented, we will become faith oriented. That's how our minds are geared; we're always trying to find answers to problems. Our minds have been so divinely created by God that they are wired to attract solutions to our problems. That's why we need to change our thinking, so that we will have more of those answers.

The Lord has millions of ways to do millions of different things; millions of ways to answer one prayer request, to fill one desire, to satisfy one longing. We need to learn how to open ourselves up to these realms of possibilities where, all of a sudden, we find ourselves bombarded with more opportunities than we know what to do with. Changing the way you think is another critical key to seeing those opportunities and hacking the Pareto Distribution.

This really makes perfect sense. If we want to extend ourselves beyond where we are, we have to learn to think beyond our current capacity. Changing how we think changes the way we see things, and also impacts the way we speak. One of the problems with changing the way we think, as I mentioned before, is that we think at two different levels, consciously and subconsciously. Our deliberate decision-making occurs at the conscious level of thinking. Our overall success, however, depends in large part to how we are thinking at our subconscious level. It is the thinking at the subconscious level that creates our everyday habits and routines. Aristotle is credited with the quote: "We are what we repeatedly do. Excellence, then, is not an act, but a habit." If this is true, then it's our subconscious thinking that really needs to be changed. And that involves changing the way our subconscious is programmed. Some have described our subconscious as the "computer code" of how we do life.

One of the solutions I've learned in changing that subconscious coding, if you will, is what I often call "the law of first mention." This concept is best-known as a way to interpret religious texts and concepts; however, the law of first mention works in our everyday lives as well. Simply stated, the law of first mention says that the way something is presented for the first time is key to understanding it every time it appears after that. From my experience in coaching and dealing with people, I have discovered that most people don't know what they like; they like what they know. We all like what we're most familiar with. This way of thinking causes certain patterns to occur in our everyday life. Even when we recognize a pattern that we don't like, we still usually continue to live in that pattern. Let me give you an example: We've all seen or known the girl or guy who is an amazing and wonderful person. They are smart, attractive, personable, successful, etc. They seem to have everything together in their lives...and yet they are constantly dating losers. They're always getting hooked up with total jerks. We see them and shake our heads, thinking that if Jane could just find a *good* guy, or if Joe could just find a *good* girl, everything would be fine. And we can't understand why it doesn't happen. So often, the issue is that when Jane *finds* a good guy or Joe, a good girl, they subconsciously sabotage the relationship because there is something they want more than a healthy relationship; in their subconscious, they want to be proven right. So, until they change their subconscious programming, everything they do will work to cause that subconscious programming to continue to be a reality. This subconscious sabotage not only occurs in

> **Sabotage not only occurs in relationships; it also happens with our money, opportunity, and success.**

relationships; it also happens with our money, opportunity, and success as well.

When dealing with the law of first mention, what we have to do first is figure out where that first mention came from. Most of the time our laws of first mention are developed while we are children, through conversations we hear, lessons we learn from our parents and other authority figures in our lives, and in our religious upbringing—whatever form that takes during childhood. Changing our subconscious coding can be particularly difficult if we have little memory of our childhood, or so many painful memories of those years that we find it too difficult or hurtful to deal with. But most of us have numerous memories of things we heard or were taught. When it comes to the area of finances, many people believe or assume that making money is very hard. Quite often, this is due to their having grown up hearing their parents or others say, "We can't afford that," or "I work too hard for what money we have just to spend it on that." As far as religious upbringing, many of us were taught from the book of Genesis that the earth will return its strength and yield to us only by hard toil and the sweat of our brow. These and other similar thoughts and words and teachings from our past impact us as adults in the form of our subconscious programming.

One of my businesses is teaching people how to trade on the stock market. We teach people how to use their money in such a way as to get better returns for every dollar they invest. It truly amazes me how many people initially enjoy great success and to turn around and subconsciously sabotage that success because they decide they're making money too *easily*. Making money isn't supposed to be easy; that's what we're told. What if I told you that you could simply push a button one day and push it again a few days later and have money appear in your account? Most people would say, "Sure! That's for me!" But how many would really believe it? We think it's too easy. It doesn't fit our definition of "work." Besides, we didn't "work" for that money; all we did was push a button. That's just it: pushing that button *was* the work needed to achieve that task. What we need to change are our definitions and what they look like in operation.

In order to change the law of first mention we must first recognize it. We must own the fact that it isn't necessarily true and then replace it with something else. For many people, this can be difficult, as most people's deepest desire is to be right in their belief systems. However, this is where the power of making declarations over your life comes into effect. When we make declarations, as we learned in the last chapter, the words we speak will create the world we walk into.

As we mentioned before, Proverbs 18:21 says, "Death and life are in the power of the tongue, And those who love it will eat its fruit." Most people don't quote the second part of that verse, but the second part of it helps us understand that if life and death are in the power of the tongue, those who love it or under-stand it, eat its fruit. In other words, what we say, we eat, because, at some point in the future, what we say becomes our new reality. This is why James says, "The tongue also is a fire, a world of evil among the parts of the body. It corrupts the whole body, sets the whole course of one's life on fire, and is itself set on fire by hell" (Jas. 3:6). But the tongue also can cause a world of blessing. Whenever we make declarations, we create new laws of first mention that supplant the old. If you are one of those people, for example, who think making money is hard, I encourage you visualize that limiting law of first mention. Visualize yourself taking a sledgehammer to it and shattering it to pieces. Then begin visualizing and declaring over yourself saying, "Making money is easy!" and framing that statement in place of the old one.

Here are a few of the financial declarations I have made and use in my own life and at home with my family:

- Making money is easy.
- Favor goes before me. Wisdom speaks to me. Might works through me.
- Because God is with me, I cannot fail.
- People love to give me money for answers I provide.
- Everything my hands touch prospers.
- It is the goodness of God to make me rich and He adds no sorrow to it.

Say these things to the average person, and they will look at you like you're crazy because those are not their laws of first mention. Everything we hear is filtered through our laws of first mention. Think about when you first learn something new. I believe it was John Maxwell who said that the first time we hear something new, we say "That can't be true." The second time we hear it, we say, "I've heard that before." The third time we hear it, we say, "I've thought that before."

Declarations are powerful because they strike at the heart of our paradigm of what we think is true. They shock us into the place where we have to grow beyond where we are to find success, because the success we desire is never in our current place. The success we want is outside of where we currently are.

Therefore, if it's the old laws holding us back, we have to replace them and create new subconscious programs that propel us forward. We do that personally by recognizing it and then by making declarations of a new law of first mention. This is the continual repetition of those declarations that really embed the new program in our thinking.

Think about someone who becomes involved in a multilevel or direct marketing business such as Amway, for example. If they have a really bad experience, they might look at it and similar businesses and say, "They're just pyramid schemes; they don't work. I'm never doing anything like that ever again"— despite the fact that hundreds of thousands of people around the world are making tons of money doing that very thing. So, is it a pyramid scheme or is it not? Is it a viable business or is it not? It depends on how people approach it, what law of first mention they bring to it.

Many people who are risk-averse likely took a risk at some point and failed, which scared them from taking any further risks. But life teaches us that in order to do something well, we first must fall down—repeatedly. Consider a child just learning to walk. They take a halting step or two, or possibly three, and then they fall down. We don't look at them and laugh and say, "Silly baby! You only took two steps." No. What do we do? We celebrate the two steps they took and ask them to do it again.

But often in business we do just the opposite to ourselves. Suppose you said to me, "Well, I started this company and it was very good and it worked for three years and then it just collapsed on top of itself. That's it; I'm never doing another business." Wait a minute. You just told me that your business worked for three years. Take what you've learned and apply it to your next business. Maybe that business will work for ten years and then you can turn around and sell it and make a lot of money. It's the repetition of the declarations that help reprogram what we want to replace as the law of first mention. That's how we actually begin changing the way we think.

So, I challenge you to sit down and take some time to think about your laws of first mention that may be holding you back. Ask yourself where you see it in your life, especially where it's related to your finances and business. Maybe it's related to the stock market because you heard someone you admire talk about losing a lot of money in the stock market. Perhaps you have a friend who lost a bundle in the 2008 market crisis, and now you are terrified to have anything to do with the market, despite the fact that there are millions of people worldwide who consistently make lots of money trading in the stock market or in real estate. Whatever it is, identify the laws of first mention that are hindering you, and replace them with declarations to form new laws of first mention that will bring you success in the future. Then, take a step of faith and act on the new laws. Take a course where you can learn how to better invest in the stock market or in real estate. You may be surprised by the success you find there!

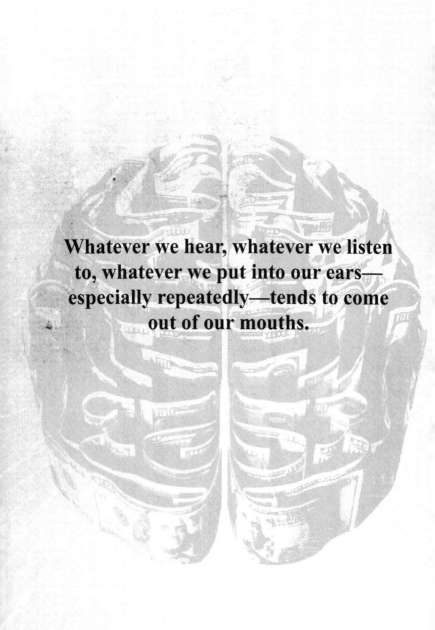

Whatever we hear, whatever we listen to, whatever we put into our ears—especially repeatedly—tends to come out of our mouths.

Chapter Five

Change the Way You Hear

While changing the way we think—replacing old, unfruitful laws of first mention with new, fruitful ones—is critical for hacking the Pareto Distribution, it is not enough. Much of our thinking is influenced by what and how we hear, so if we are hearing the wrong way, or hearing the wrong things, we can try to change our thinking, but those other noises can impede our progress. So, we must be ready to change the way we hear. That is the fourth, indispensable key to unlocking the Matthew Effect into our lives.

Luke records in his Gospel two statements of Jesus that speak to the importance of being careful how we hear, and how we listen. Both occur in the 18th chapter of Luke. The first of Jesus' statements appears in the context of his parable of the sower and the seed. A farmer sows seed in his field, which represents the preaching of the gospel of the kingdom of God. Jesus describes four different kinds of soil and how they respond to the seed. The soils represent the different ways people respond to the gospel message; in other words, how they *hear* that message. Those responses range from full rejection to full acceptance...of the *same message*. Then Jesus says, "Whoever has ears to hear, let them hear" (Lk. 8:8d). His point is that not everyone who can hear with their ears can hear with understanding.

Jesus' second statement about hearing occurs in a shorter parable that immediately follows the first one: "No one lights a lamp and hides it in a clay jar or puts it under a bed. Instead, they put it on a stand, so that those who come in can see the light. For there is nothing hidden that will not be disclosed, and nothing concealed that will not be known or brought out into the open. Therefore *consider carefully how you listen*. Whoever has will be given more; whoever does not have, even what they think they have will be taken from them" (Lk. 8:16-18, emphasis added).

In Mark's version of the same parable of the lamp, Jesus' words are slightly different: "'Consider carefully what you hear,' he continued. 'With the measure you use, it will be measured to you—and even more. Whoever has will be given more; whoever does not have, even what they have will be taken from them'" (Mark 4:25). What he's saying here is that whatever we measure out and give to others is what we will receive back in proportion and even more. Being careful about what and how we hear—and about changing how we hear when necessary—is very important because faith (our fifth key for unlocking the Matthew Effect) comes by hearing: "So then faith *comes* by hearing, and hearing by the word of God" (Rom. 10:17 NKJV). Key four, changing our hearing, and key five, faith, are interlocked with one another.

Whatever we hear, whatever we listen to, whatever we put into our ears, especially repeatedly, tends to come out of our mouths. And remember, the words we speak can either bless or curse, help or hinder, build up or tear down.

I have four little boys. They are like sponges; they listen to and picks up everything. Most of the time that's good, if they're hearing positive things. Other times, like when I stub my toe, it's not so good.

That's why their mother and I have to be very careful what we say around them, because our words become a reality that we're framing up around them that they're going to step into and live with. Whatever they hear us say, they not only say, but repeat and believe. It's the same way with us: what we hear, eventually gets deep inside us and that is what eventually comes out of our mouths. So, if we listen to negative people, we will think and say negative things. If we listen to people who are always talking about lack and not having enough, or fearmongering (the media are *masters* at that!), then we will think and speak the same way, and that is what will manifest in our lives. That's why I don't listen to much news and media; just enough to stay up-to-date with current events. Most of it is far too negative. In fact, I have learned that the vast majority of people only listen to people who sound like them or echo their viewpoints. We see it all the time, whether it be videos on social media, our "favorite" network news stations in traditional news media, or even our friends' conversations. If we are not careful, this confirmation bias will keep us stagnant in the very areas of our lives (relational, financial, physical, etc.) where we say we want progress because it will reinforce the very worldview from which we are so desperate to break free.

> **Confirmation bias will keep us stagnant in the very areas of our lives (relational, financial, physical, etc.) where we say we want progress.**

Since faith comes from hearing, we must take care of how we hear and listen, because what we hear will create more faith for it to manifest in our life. So, when we hear such things as "The rich get richer, but that's not for me," and really listen to it, we actually take away from ourselves opportunities to grow and advance. We cut ourselves off from stepping into being the rich who get richer. But when we hear, "The rich get richer" and ask, "Okay, how do *I* become rich? What are some ways I can get into this law? What are some ways I can insert myself into this effect so that I get the benefits of this spiritual law coming into my life?"...the door opens for us to step into it.

So, when Jesus says, "Consider carefully what you hear," we need to understand that the issue is not so much what we hear as how we hear it. We may all hear the same words spoken, but we each may "hear" something different as to meaning or intent in those words. And that could lead to misunderstanding. A great example of this in the Bible is in Numbers 13. In this chapter, Moses has sent spies into the land of Canaan to "'See what the land is like, and whether the people who live in it are strong or weak, whether they are few or many. And how is the land in which they live, is it good or bad? And how are the cities in which they live, are the people in open camps or in fortifications? And how is the land, is it productive or unproductive? Are there trees in it or not? And show yourselves courageous and get some of the fruit of the land.' Now the time was the season of the first ripe grapes" (Num 13:18-20 NASB). Scripture says that when they returned, they gave a good report of the land. Caleb said, "'We should by all means go up and take possession of it, for we will certainly prevail over it.' But the men who had gone up with him said, 'We are not able to go up against the people, because they are too strong for us'" (Num 13:30-31 NASB). Later, in the New Testament, Hebrews says that those in the wilderness in Numbers 13 had good news shared with them, but the news they heard did not benefit them, because it was not mixed with faith in those who heard it (Heb 4:2). How many times has this happened in our own lives? We hear something that could be wonderful, but we hear it wrong, or we don't mix it with faith, and we miss what could have been a huge blessing.

One of the best life experience examples of this is a marriage or other deeply committed relationship. How many times has your spouse or your significant other said something to you that may be as innocent as, "That shirt looks good on you," but what you *hear* is, "What...my other shirts look bad? You must think I'm ugly." We all know it happens. The question is why.

One reason for this is because we all have "ear-muffs" through which we filter everything we hear.

This has some to do with the law of first mention that we talked about in chapter four, but it also has a lot to do with our self-talk and how we view ourselves. If you view yourself as someone who is "less than," you have a hard time receiving a compliment from someone, regardless of their sincerity, because you don't really believe it. This filtering tendency shows up in the way we relate to everything we do in the world. Whether it's politics, business, workplace, family, church, synagogue, mosque, or wherever, we filter everything we hear through our own personal set of "earmuffs" that are set to our particular prejudices, assumptions, and expectations. For this reason, we must learn to listen truly and carefully so we can know and act according to what someone actually said rather than what we think they said.

This can open up lucrative opportunities in the business world. One thing I have learned as an entrepreneur is that when I hear of a "problem" someone has, I don't hear it as a problem but as an opportunity. I realized in business long ago that if you can solve people's problems, they will pay you a lot of money to do it. So, whenever you see someone with an issue or a problem, if you can find a solution for that problem, you may have the potential of a successful business on your hands.

Think of it this way: *An opportunity always comes to us wrapped in the packaging of a problem.* Otherwise, there is

An opportunity always comes to us wrapped in the packaging of a problem.

no opportunity. If you had all the money you wanted in your bank account, and it had been given to you, then you would never have the opportunity (or the need) to create a business to generate extra income, because you wouldn't have the problem of wanting or needing to make more money. If you're fine with where you are, why would you do anything else?

In 2020, brick-and-mortar businesses confronted a big problem called COVID-19. But many entrepreneurs saw this "problem" as an opportunity to change the way they do business. Churches saw the opportunity to start doing more virtual meetings, tent-meetings, and home group-style events. Restaurants saw the opportunity to start doing more outdoor dining. New entrepreneurs launched new services to help do business remote or from home. There are all sorts of opportunities wrapped up in problems, but we will rarely see those opportunities if all we're thinking about is the problem.

So, when we're looking at this key, we have to learn to hear what's being said through a different filter than we're

> **What we listen to repeatedly gives us faith for it to happen.**

used to. We have to hear it differently, beyond the surface or fundamental issue that's being proposed. Again, scripture says that faith comes by hearing. So, we need to be careful not only what we listen to, but also how we listen to it, because what we listen to repeatedly gives us faith for it to happen. This is where declarations can come in. When we make declarations, especially daily, we start decreeing new things, new behaviors, new opportunities over our lives, we begin taking our earmuffs off.

Let me give you an example of how this works in a relationship. Like most couples, my wife and I have had plenty of disagreements and misunderstandings, but we have a firm agreement on two fundamental principles. Number one, we love each other, and number two, we only want to see the best manifest in one another. So, whenever she says something to me that triggers or upsets me, I have already established within myself that she loves me and would never intentionally hurt me because she wants to see the best come out of me. We've had sit-down conversations (BEFORE a fight ever happens) where we decided, "If I say something to you that hurts you or upsets you, I'm not intentionally harming you, so if it comes across that way, please ask me about it."

With this understanding established, if she says something to me that hurts my feelings, or triggers me in some way, I know I can go to her and say, "Hey, when you said what you said, this is what I heard. This is how I took it. How did you actually mean for this to come across?" That allows us to have a healthy, air-clearing conversation that doesn't blow up into anger and resentment where we don't talk to each other for two or three days. And it's all because we share a paradigm in which we both affirm, "I love you, and I know that you love me and that you would never intentionally hurt me." That has become our law of first mention.

Building that kind of relationship and understanding takes time and practice. A *whole lot* of practice. It also takes a willingness to take responsibility. Being responsible for something does not mean taking the blame for something that isn't your fault. It just means that you are taking responsibility to change it rather than becoming a victim from it. One of my old mentors once told me, "Mark, you have the life you want right now by results, otherwise you would have a different life." At the time, I had lost my job due to the housing crash in 2007-2008 and was single, broke, and feeling helpless. However, this shifted my mindset, that if I have chosen where I am at, I can choose where I want to go from here. If I'm a victim of my circumstances, it doesn't matter what level of success I attain in any area because a circumstance over which I have zero control can come and mess things up again. This mindset causes deep anxiety and frustration in our mental health. However, if I am responsible for my life, I can live with more confidence and change the trajectory it takes. You see, taking responsibility for something actually empowers you to bring change to that thing. A relationship pastor I know, during a marital enrichment class, posed the question: "How many of you has a spouse who has at one point hurt your feelings? Every hand went up in the group of seventy-five to one hundred. "Great," he said. Then he asked, "How many of you believe that sometime over the next year or the rest of your lifetime, that your spouse will say something to you that will hurt your feelings?" Once again, everyone raised their hand. He said, "Awesome. Now, how many of you have a plan on how you will respond when that happens?" This time, almost no hands went up. That shouldn't surprise us. Most of us don't have responses; we have reactions.

There's a huge difference between a reaction and a response. A response is what people do who are trained for a situation. A reaction is what everyone else does. Here's an example. Think about a police officer who's in a bank. If an armed robber comes in and shoots a bullet into the ceiling, 99 percent of the people in that place will fall on the ground and try to hide. That's a reaction, and a perfectly natural one. The police officer, however, will move into a conditioned response mechanism rather than a reaction and take some form of action appropriate to a bank robbery scenario. Why? Because that's the way he or she has been trained.

Likewise, we have to train ourselves to hear differently, not the problem of hurt feelings, societal decline, and financial issues, but the opportunity to grow to the place where we don't get upset with our spouse, where we see how we can better impact our community, and how we can create financial opportunities for us to step into. Whether in domestic relationships, business relationships, or life in general, we have to learn how to change how we hear and what we hear so that we not only understand what was really said, but what was really meant. And that takes time, repetition, practice, and *patience*. As you work on developing this skill, give yourself grace. Like the baby learning to walk, you too will initially fail in this effort, but you will gain strength and eventually be walking in no time!

In fact, we want to help you get this process started. We want to give you a FREE list of declarations that we have used (and still do) that have helped us change the way we perceive opportunity and hear things around us. We believe this tool will help you on your journey to do the same thing.

Just visit our website for a free list here: https://www.neostrading.com/declarations-download/

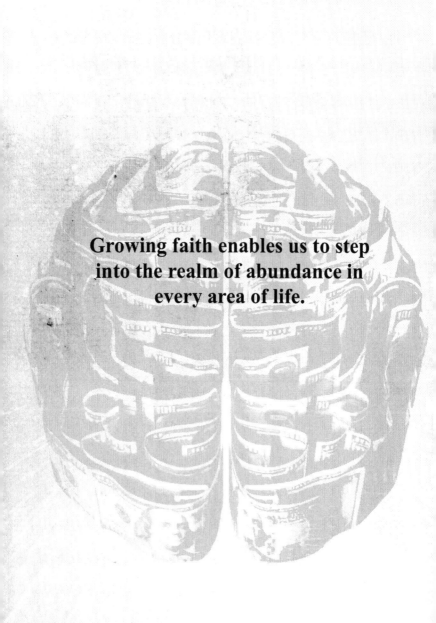

Growing faith enables us to step into the realm of abundance in every area of life.

Chapter Six

Faith

In the previous chapter, I mentioned briefly the connection between faith and hearing, and how faith comes from hearing; specifically, hearing the word of God (Rom. 10:17). Having dealt in that chapter with the critical key of changing the way we hear, it's time in this chapter to look closely at faith, the fifth vital key to hacking the Pareto Distribution. This raises a couple of questions: First, *how* does faith come from hearing? Or, to put it another way, how does hearing the right way *produce* faith. And second, what is faith and how does it work, especially in the context of activating the Matthew Effect and building wealth?

Faith comes by hearing; we need to learn to use our ears as well as our minds. Reading the word of God is important, but hearing it as well is even better because it involves more of our senses. For myself, I know that what comes out of me most often is what I have put inside me or allowed to get inside. More than just what I think or say, it is what I have heard, or seen, or experienced. Because I want those things always to be as positive as possible, I try to surround myself with abundance, to hang out with people who talk and use abundant words and who observe a life-style of generosity and gratitude. If all you ever hear is negativity, the faith that gets produced will bring negative fruit, and it will be much harder for you to achieve your dreams.

I had to learn this lesson myself, and what a huge difference it made! Much of the credit for the break-through in my life regarding this topic I give to my wife, Kate, for helping me learn it. In my earlier days of stock trading, I was caught up, almost obsessed with *how* I dealt with a trade, how much money I made, and always thinking it was not enough. Let's say that I entered a stock trade and made 15 percent, only to watch the stock rise higher to where I could have made 30 percent. I'd go to Kate feeling depressed and say, "Well, I made 15 per-cent, but I could have made 30 percent." My problem was that I was focused on the *lack*, the additional 15 per-cent I didn't have, rather than the initial 15 percent I did have. Kate helped to set my mind straight. "Well, praise the Lord for the 15 percent! Praise the Lord for the win! How many have you won in a row now? How are we doing overall now?" As I began to listen to her, she spoke life into me, then I began to declare it for myself. This slight redirection along with her words of abun-dance planted seeds in my mind, which grew faith in my heart. Why? Because faith comes by hearing. Growing faith enables us to step into the realm of abundance in every area of life—business and beyond.

Faith grows or withers depending on the people and things we surround ourselves with. When we sur-round ourselves with toxic people and continually ingest toxicity in our lives, then it shouldn't surprise us when our life becomes toxic. The opposite is just as true. If we fill our minds with positive things, inspirational books, motivational writings, the word of God, and if we surround ourselves with positive people, positivity will govern our mindset and faith will grow, which will lead to greater abundance and positivity.

A lady once asked Zig Ziglar why he focused so heavily on daily positive self-help and self-attitude. He responded by saying something to the effect of, "Why do you take a bath every day? Because usually at the end of the day you are dirty and need it. It's the same thing with our mind. I try to program my mind with positive reinforcement every day because the world can be a hard and discouraging place." The good and positive things we hear and listen to create faith inside of us so that we can believe and receive and step into those ideas—even if they haven't materialized in our lives yet.

Walking in faith is when we can create in our subconscious a reality that we are not fully experiencing yet, but live as if we are, not in fantasy, but in expectation. Hebrews 11:1 says, "Now faith is the substance of things hoped for, the evidence of things not seen" (NKJV). One example of "evidence of things not seen" is what we can see in our heads; *visualizing* where we want to be and how we're going to get there. Picking up this book is an act of faith if you believe it will help you achieve the personal goals you are visualizing. Maybe you want to be a millionaire but have no idea how to begin building toward that. Maybe you want to be a stock trader but don't know how to get started. The best way to begin is by visualizing your goal in your mind, imagining yourself doing and walking in the very thing you're dreaming of. Visualization is a vital early step of faith we must take if we are to reach our goals and realize our dreams.

> **Visualization is a vital early step of faith.**

Children are masters at using their imagination, and somewhere along the way, they are often discouraged from doing it. However, there are loads of kids who "played" at becoming a doctor, nurse, scientist, musician, and then grew up to become that very thing. We must "play" at having the life that we are wanting to create for ourselves because our subconscious can't distinguish real from fake. Bruce Lee once said, "Don't speak negatively about yourself, even as a joke. Your body doesn't know the difference."

Many people try to please God with their behavior, but that never works. Only faith pleases God: "But without faith it is impossible to please [God], for he who comes to God must believe that He is, and that He is a rewarder of those who diligently seek Him" (Heb. 11:6 NKJV). It's not our behavior, but our faith, that pleases God. This verse tells us that in order to please God, we must exercise faith in two ways: 1) we must believe that God *is*—that He exists—and 2) that God *rewards* those who diligently seek him.

"Diligently seek him" is another way of saying "walk by faith." All these actions we take, whether visualizing, writing down our goals, declaring our goals, or role-playing our goals, are acts of faith that we do to help bring the future into our reality. This is the working out of the substance of things not seen. We're creating a substance of something we haven't seen that will become our future reality that we get to step into. So, when we want to put ourselves in the Pareto Distribution where the rich are getting richer, we visualize ourselves gaining and using wealth. We visualize ourselves gaining status. We visualize ourselves having money come to us. We make declarations over our lives. Here is a great key: view yourself as already being rich or wealthy, because the truth is you are! If the rich are getting richer, and you are already "rich," then these principles must work to help bring you more opportunity to grow in your wealth.

Faith is a confident expectation based on trust in a reliable party. Faith is going to the bus stop at a certain time, expecting the bus to be on schedule. Jesus said that whoever wants to enter the kingdom of God must come with the faith of a child (Matt. 18:3; Lk. 18:17). He wasn't talking about child-ish faith, but child-like faith. Having faith like a child does not mean being gullible or trusting blindly regardless of who is speaking. It means trusting that we live in a realm of infinite possibilities where anything and everything is possible merely because we believe in it, because we have not allowed the disappointments of life to take root in our hearts. It means living in a constant place of hope, where truly anything is possible to him who believes. Until taught otherwise by their parents or life experiences, children usually trust anyone. If my children climb on something or are stuck on something, they will eagerly jump into my arms because they know Daddy will catch him. But they also may jump into the arms of a stranger because they believe anyone will catch them. That's a child's innate sense and desire of adventure. Children live in a realm of infinite possibility because life hasn't taught them disappointment yet.

Anything and everything is possible merely because we believe in it.

And there's the rub. As adults, all of us have had our share of disappointments, whether in relationships, business, career aspirations, dream fulfillment, or whatever. We've had disappointments in money ventures, and any of these disappointments can take root in our hearts and cause us to come against that childlike faith. That's what we have to deal with. But how do we do it? We do it by realizing—and reminding ourselves as often as necessary—that just because we suffered disappointment in the past over a particular issue or situation doesn't necessarily mean it will continue to happen in the future. It's often easier to continue believing in the failures of the past than to believe in the successes of the future. It's the ones who believe in that success regardless of past failures (no matter how many) that achieve success. Consider Thomas Edison. After literally thousands of failures in the attempt, it would have been easier for him to believe that he would never invent the light bulb. But he kept on believing, and kept on trying, and finally succeeded. How easy it would have been for Abraham Lincoln to give up on running for public office after losing in his first several attempts. But he kept on believing, and kept on trying, and finally was elected President of the United States just in time to navigate the nation through the upheaval of the Civil War.

However, disappointment is a fierce foe we must overcome to achieve our goals. We have to fully believe that the desires in our heart and the dreams in our minds are worth fighting for regardless. Scripture says, "But for him who is joined to all the living there is hope, for a living dog is better than a dead lion" (Ecclesiastes 9:4 NKJV). If there is breath in your lungs, there is hope for your goals and desires to become a reality. As I mentioned though, it's far easier to create a paradigm of expectation based on what happened in our past than it is to look forward to what we could create in the future. For example, let's say you've been trading in stocks and your last two or three trades didn't work out. It would be natural for you to think that the next one won't work out either. If you were to keep on thinking or believing that way, it could very well become a self-fulfilling prophecy. You start living in fear, which short-circuits faith. But suppose you have adopted the paradigm that past failures don't necessarily determine future results. So, you try another trade, and this time it works. And it works the next time, and the next, and the next. You begin manifesting what you have, in faith, believed.

> **Past failures don't necessarily determine future results.**

Proverbs 13:12 says, "Hope deferred makes the heart sick, but when the desire comes, it is a tree of life" (NKJV). Many people who know and love the first part of that verse are unfamiliar with the rest of it. The phrase "tree of life" appears only a few times in the Bible, so whenever it appears, it is significant. Although we may become heartsick at the delay in our dreams, hope realized—"when the desire comes"—becomes a tree of life growing strong and vibrant within us.

Being negative is easy. It doesn't take faith to focus on the negatives. That's the natural course of life. If it changes, it's because we take the initiative. We have to take action. The Second Law of Thermodynamics states that anything left unattended will deteriorate. That law says that if I leave a piece of bare metal outside, it will rust. Faith says that if I leave a piece of metal outside, it won't rust. However, acting on my faith says that I will need to spray the metal with Rust-Oleum paint to take care of it so that it will not rust. So, we must have faith, but we also must act on our faith or it has no power. Remember, James 2:20 says that "faith without works is useless." Real faith spurs us to action.

It's natural to fear failure and disappointment. Many people are afraid to hope because their hopes have been dashed too many times in the past, and they don't want to go through that kind of pain again. But failure is actually the only way that we grow. We see this throughout life. Toddlers learn to walk by falling (frequently). They take two or three steps and fall, but they get up and go again, taking maybe five or six steps before falling again. But who would look at a toddler walking and falling and laugh, and say, "Silly baby, you can't even walk right"? No one. Rather, we would celebrate the progress that toddler was making. Though falling, that toddler was learning, and, after getting up, would press on, better than before. That's progress. It's the same with learning to ride a bike. No one ever learns to ride a bike without at least a few falls and skinned knees. We fall, and it hurts, but we get back up and, after some Bactine and a Band-Aid, we're right back on that bike and trying again. And we keep at it until we master it.

Why don't we have the same attitude when it comes to business, or building wealth, or in our relationships? A few disappointments or setbacks or conflicts, and we're ready to hang it all up. Instead of giving up, we need to learn from our disappointments so we can grow. Let me share a personal story to illustrate this. When Kate and I first got married, one of the ways I dealt with conflict was to shut down. I would simply leave the conversation for a period of time so I could think about what I wanted to say because I didn't want to say anything terrible out of anger or frustration.

Then I would come back to it. My problem was that it would usually take me a couple of days to come back to it. Kate, on the other hand, was the type of person who wanted to resolve her stuff by talking it out in that moment. So, early in our marriage, if we had a fight, I would walk away and not talk about it for a day...and it drove Kate nuts.

Over the years, I've grown. I still walk away, but now it's only for two minutes, and then I'm back to resolve the issue. I'll walk out of the room, gather my thoughts, come back in, and boom—we talk it out. Kate is great about it. Instead of saying something like, "I can't believe that after all this time you still have to walk away from a conversation," she says, "Look how much progress you've made, compared to where you used to be. You couldn't talk about this conversation for a full day and now it only takes you a couple of minutes."

Sara Blakely, who is the founder and CEO of Spanx, has said that her father trained her and her brother to think differently about what success looks like. He encouraged them to fail. She said that around the dinner table, he would ask them, "What did you try new today that you didn't succeed at?" He wanted them to learn not to be afraid to try new things and explore new avenues and ventures. She says the lesson was that failure is not about the outcome, for true failure is not trying. For me, failure in any endeavor only occurs if I don't try or don't learn from the undertaking. Success then has two faces. The first, and often less valuable, is achieving my desired outcome; the second is what I've learned after I've failed at something. With this mindset, I am now always learning and always succeeding!

I believe that emphasizing success and progress with others and encouraging them to learn from their failures, rather than harping on them, is one of the best ways to inspire faith and "abundance" thinking in those around us. We all want to be surrounded with hope-filled and encouraging people, so why not become one yourself? By doing this, you will begin to create a culture of faith and success around you and then, hopefully, people will begin to see these things manifest in their lives rather than keeping them shackled to their past.

I would encourage you even now to begin looking toward your future with hope and expectation. Come into agreement with what the LORD says in Jeremiah 29:11: "For I know the plans that I have for you,' declares the Lord, 'plans for prosperity and not for disaster, to give you a future and a hope." Have faith that the plans of the LORD will come about. So let me ask you, what do you want to create? Don't worry about "how" you'll do it, but focus on what you want and WHY you want it. Then, let me challenge you to visualize yourself obtaining that goal. If you are serious about this, you can go to our website and download a free tool that will help you through this process. I look forward to seeing your imagination come to life!

Faithful stewardship opens doors because if you're faithful with a little, you'll be entrusted with a lot.

Chapter Seven

Stewardship

The sixth and final, critical key for unlocking the Matthew Effect is stewardship. I hear some of you now saying, "Wait a minute, Mark! Isn't stewardship just another word for giving? You talked about giving in chapter two." That's right, I did. However, while giving is part of stewardship, there is considerably more to stewardship than just giving. In fact, you could say that stewardship encompasses all of the previous five keys and is the culmination of them, because stewardship relates to the whole of life, not just one part of it. Good stewardship is the demonstration and practice of wise management skills, and thus puts us into a place where we can receive abundance. There are many scriptures that teach this truth. One of the key scriptures for me is Luke 16:10-11, where Jesus says, "Whoever can be trusted with very little can also be trusted with much, and whoever is dishonest with very little will also be dishonest with much. So if you have not been trustworthy in handling worldly wealth, who will trust you with true riches?" It makes perfect sense. If you are faithful with the little you have been given—if you consider the little important enough to take care of properly—you will show that you can be trusted to take care of larger amounts. But if you are careless and irresponsible with other people's assets that have been placed in your trust, why should you expect to be given your own assets to squander?

We actually see this principle played out in the lives of the Old Testament prophets Elijah and Elisha. Elijah was a powerful prophet of God, and Elisha was his servant and assistant. Wherever Elijah went, Elisha went and faithfully served the prophet. Elisha refused to leave Elijah's side. Finally, on the day when they both knew that Elijah was going to be taken up into heaven, he asked Elisha, When they had crossed over, Elijah said to Elisha, "Ask me what I should do for you before I am taken from you." And Elisha said, "Please let a double portion of your spirit be upon me." (2 Ki. 2:9). Elisha received his request and became an even greater miracle-working prophet than Elijah. Before that happened, however, Elisha "paid his dues," so to speak, by faithful, often menial service to Elijah.

One of the most powerful statements in the Bible about stewardship, at least to me, involves Elisha and is found in Second Kings chapter three. Joram, the king of Israel, Jehoshaphat, the king of Judah, and the unnamed king of Edom have allied together to war against Mesha, the king of Moab, who has rebelled against paying his regular tribute to Joram, king of Israel. At one point, when the three kings and their armies are without water, Jehoshaphat desires counsel from a prophet: "But Jehoshaphat asked, 'Is there no prophet of the LORD here, through whom we may

inquire of the LORD?' An officer of the king of Israel
But Jehoshaphat said, "Is there no prophet of the Lord
here, that we may inquire of the Lord by him?" And
one of the king of Israel's servants answered and said,
"Elisha the son of Shaphat is here, who used to pour
water on the hands of Elijah." And Jehoshaphat said,
"The word of the Lord is with him. (2 Ki. 3:11-12a
emphasis added). Here was a prophet who was greater
than Elijah, a prophet who received a double portion
of Elijah's spirit. By this time in his life, Elisha had
parted the waters of the Jordan River in order to cross,
purified deadly waters, and commanded nature, yet he
was better known as the one who "used to pour water
on the hands of Elijah." Elisha was as famous for
his servitude—his stewardship—to Elijah as for his
prophetic gifts and power. Elisha received a "double
portion" of Elijah's spirit, but before that, he was the
prophet's faithful servant. His example shows us the
power of stewardship (along with the proper servant
spirit) to place us in the position to receive our own.

Maybe you're saying to yourself, "But Mark, I
don't have anything to be faithful over." Of course, you
do! Do you have a job? Then be the best employee you
can possibly be. One of my mentors in life once told
me, "Find the job no one wants to do and do it. Eventually, people will notice and you'll get rewarded."
What about your family? Your friends? Be a steward
to them by treating them well and by looking for ways
to encourage and bless them, and, in Paul's words, "but
with humility consider one another as more important
than yourselves; do not merely look out for your own

personal interests, but also for the interests of others."
(Phil. 2:3b-4). Be a steward at your church, vacuum-
ing or cleaning or helping out in any way you can,
no matter how menial it may seem—and perform it
as though it was the most important job in the world.
Always be looking for ways you can serve more and
serve better. Jesus set the example as one who came
not to be served, but to serve (Matt. 20:28). Faithful
stewardship opens doors. So, whatever you do, do it
unto the Lord as a memorial, and let that stewardship
bring returns, because, if you're faithful with a little,
you'll be entrusted with a lot.

The fact that I have my own stock trading education company today is because I was faithful with the
vision of another individual under whom I served. I
served at another trading education company for over
a decade, teaching their courses, developing content for them, and helping to push and promote that
company in any way that I could. I fully believe that
because I was faithful in that, in return, the Lord has
given us our own business and has blessed it tremen-
dously. Being faithful, or being a good steward, brings
everything together—giving, gratitude, changing the
way we think and hear, and faith—and sets us up to
begin inserting ourselves into the Pareto Distribution.

One of the reasons that stewardship, in the sense
of taking good care of someone else's stuff, opens the
door for you to have more, is because it is so counterintuitive to our culture. Most people automatically
care for their own things more than they do someone
else's things. Take renting a car, for example. Many

people do not take care of rental cars as carefully as they do their own. They tend to drive faster than in their own car, although usually not dangerously so, if for no other reason than not wanting to pay the insurance if something goes wrong. But they neglect care in other ways. Maybe they would never dream of eating in their own car or strewing trash throughout the vehicle—but don't think twice about doing those things in a rental. After all, the rental companies have people whose job is to clean up the cars after they're returned. So why bother?

Good stewardship demonstrates not only maturity and responsibility but, most importantly, character. Aside from being a spiritual principle, it is simple

> **Good stewardship demonstrates maturity, responsibility, and most importantly, character.**

common sense not to entrust much to someone who has not shown wisdom and faithfulness with a little. We all get opportunities in life to serve others, and those service opportunities, I believe, are tests to see how well we will do when dealing with our own stuff. That's the lesson of Elisha: he served Elijah so faithfully and so well that even after he became, in many ways, a greater prophet than Elijah, he was still known as the one who had washed Elijah's hands.

The quality and effectiveness of service towards others depends on our attitude, on our view as to the how and why of what we're doing, and of who we're doing it for. Maybe we do it out of love; perhaps we do it out of compassion for someone who needs help for a time; or maybe we do it for the simple joy that comes in doing good to others. Whatever the reason, try, to view your service as a "trade" into that individual or that business that will reap a return for you. Stewardship, at its heart, is about managing something well that belongs to someone else. Wise and faithful stewards will eventually reap a "harvest," because the one who entrusted his or her things to us will be very grateful and will reward us for our stewardship. This, in fact, is just what Jesus promises in the scriptures we looked at earlier as well as in others.

So, if I view this as a trade, I'm not going to trade on a stock without the likelihood of a reward; that would be senseless, not to mention poor stewardship. One of our guidelines in trading is to take only trades where the potential return greatly outweighs the risk involved. I won't get into a trade where I risk ten to make one. There's a high probability that I would lose all ten and gain nothing. Instead, I will get into a trade where, for example, I risk 3 percent for the chance to make 7 percent. So, if I'm right, I'm making double my risk. And even if I lose on one, I make money on another.

Stewardship involves both money and mindset. Let's use an example from the workplace. Suppose a person is a hard worker at their job, always busting their tail trying to do their best, and always looking for ways to improve. Their boss probably is going to take notice. And if they're a good steward over that job, chances are they're going to get promoted. In fact, my spiritual father, Vin, once told me that when he was up for a raise to become, at the time, the youngest VP at JP Morgan, he was told at the interview it was a formality because he was already acting as a VP and they were just rewarding him for what he had already been doing for the last six months. You see, most people want the title, the promotion, and the pay structure first, but often, we get those things AFTER we step into that role and do those tasks. That's a positive return: good stewardship with little reward often results in being entrusted with more. The same principle works when managing our personal finances. Being a good steward over your money means that you take care of it, you aren't frivolous with it, that you have a plan for it, and that you execute that plan. Do all of that consistently, and eventually things will begin to add up. I heard a saying one time that if you don't have a plan for your money, someone else does. It's so true. Money always flows to a plan, whether yours or someone else's.

Money always flows to a plan, whether yours or someone else's.

So be sure to have a plan for your money that includes realistic allocations for bills, necessities, investing, saving, vacations, discretionary spending, etc. Then, start executing that plan and stick with it, making adjustments along the way as needed. As you're faithful with that plan over time, your money will grow, everything else will start to snowball, and you will become wealthier and wealthier. I constantly tell my trading students that when you take a trade in a stock, the most important thing you can do is have a plan on how you will manage that position BEFORE you enter the trade. Scripture even says that "The plans of the diligent lead surely to abundance, but everyone who is hasty comes only to poverty" (Prov 21:5 ESV). Whether we're talking about money or about life, stewardship works, and we really can't go wrong with it. Whenever I serve someone, my goal is that in the end, the person I serve will be appreciative and feel valued. In my heart, I place a demand on that service and expect a return, benefit, or a reward to come back to me. Even if the person I am serving doesn't reward me, my service as a steward to that person is never wasted. If our stewardship is for the Lord as well as for others, the Lord will reward us even if the people we serve do not. And no one can outgive the Lord. So, when we act as a steward—when we take care of someone else's stuff (business, money, etc), and do it well and with a good spirit—I truly believe that it opens a door for the opportunity for us to receive our own reward. I am a living testimony of that!

Let me encourage you now to take a moment and think about some ways you can step into greater levels of stewardship over your business or job. How can you become a better steward in your relationships with your spouse, children, friends, or significant other? How can you become a better steward of your finances and investments? If you are interested in some support, especially on the latter, please visit www.neoscdg.com where you can request a FREE consultation to see if our education system can help take your investments to the next level, as it has so many of our other students.

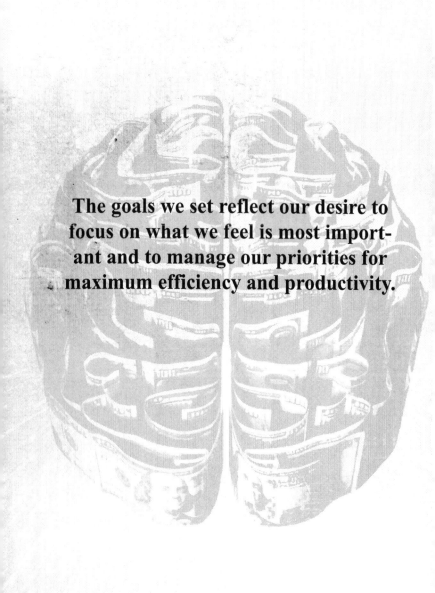

The goals we set reflect our desire to focus on what we feel is most important and to manage our priorities for maximum efficiency and productivity.

Chapter Eight

Goals and Declarations

I briefly discussed the power of declaration in chapter four, on the importance of changing the way we think, but it's such an important concept that I want to conclude this book by unpacking it in greater detail—why and the wherefore of declarations, in relation to writing and setting goals. There is power in writing goals and there is power in declaring goals, but there is compounded power in both writing *and* declaring goals; and the more often you declare your goals, the better.

I remember reading a university study regarding goal setting. The study found that between writing and declaring goals, people who speak their declarations out loud one time have a 25 percent likelihood of achieving them over a certain time frame. That likelihood jumps to 42 percent for people who simply write down their declarations on a regular basis.[5] The most amazing discovery was that people who both write down and speak their declarations, *and speak them*

---

[5] https://www.huffpost.com/entry/the-power-of-writing-down_b_12002348

every day, have over a whopping 90 percent probability of achieving their goals! That's pretty profound.
So, if that inspires you (it certainly inspires me), let's
talk about setting goals and writing them down. Then
we'll discuss how to apply our imagination and focus
our energies for even greater impact in realizing our
goals.

The goals we set, quite often, reflect our desire to
focus on what we feel is most important, and to manage our priorities for maximum efficiency and productivity. There's nothing wrong with that, as far as it goes.
However, the greatest impact comes when we tie our
goals to a bigger and greater purpose. The difference
between the two lies with the intention of our heart. For
example, one of my bigger purposes or visions is to be
the best father on the planet. I want my children, when
they're grown, to say, "We had the best dad ever." I
want to set a paradigm for them on what it means to
be, not just a good father, but a good man. So, one of
the things I do in service of that vision is get up and
cook breakfast every morning. It would be easy to see
cooking breakfast as a menial and mundane task if
separated from the bigger, overarching goal. What's
my reason for cooking breakfast? My kids need to be
fed. But another reason is that I want them to see Dad
taking care of them, to see Dad helping, to see that
it's not just Mom. I want them to know and embrace a
new paradigm for Dad. So, the mundane task of fixing
breakfast is actually a vital part of a greater and more
profound purpose. When we grab hold of that bigger
picture, whatever it is, then the tasks we create, the
goals we set accordingly, help push us into that vision.

Let's say that your goal is to be wealthy, and to work toward that goal you start cutting expenses in order to save money. That's a great start, but why are you saving money in order to become wealthy, especially if you're simply putting it in the bank, where you'll only get half a percent a year? If you're cutting expenses, why not eliminate your cable bill, keeping only your internet, and adding only specific services you will actually use, such as Netflix, Disney, Hulu, Amazon, or the like? Then take the money you save from your cable bill every month—let's say, $150—and invest it in an asset that will give a greater return like stocks or real estate or use it to pay off other existing debt. That way you have a bigger purpose for freeing up your money than just saving. We have to have an emotional, underlying purpose to what we're doing; otherwise, we'll burn out and likely never see our goals become reality.

If you're not in the habit of thinking through and writing down goals, now is the time to start. They need to be challenging yet achievable. Media icon Steve Harvey encourages people to write down 300 goals. I think that's fantastic, but I also think it can be overwhelming for people to speak 300 goals every morning and every night. What I do is encourage people to write down those 300 goals and read them all regularly over the course of a week or a month but choose three to five goals to focus on every day until they are achieved.

For myself, I have a journal in which I have written down 300 things I want to see accomplished. Some of them build on one another. For example, one of my goals is to be a billionaire. In order to become a billionaire, I first have to make $500 million, but to do that, I have to make $100 million, and to do that, I have to make $50 million and so forth. So, I have these stairstep goals (seven in all) for reaching my overarching goal of becoming a billionaire. I also own some investment property, with the big goal of eventually having at least twenty-five investment properties that will pay me $300,000 a year in income, or, roughly, $1,000 a month per property.

Writing down goals is extremely important for anything you want to achieve in life, not just in building wealth. In fact, I don't know any successful person who doesn't write down *and declare* their goals, which goes one step beyond just writing them. If writing down 300 goals seems too daunting for you, start anyway and keep pressing through, no matter how long it takes. Eventually, you'll start thinking outside of yourself, and instead of just goals for your life, you'll have goals for your business, goals for your family, and even goals for helping other people and for impacting your community. Try to be specific with your goals, because the more specific your goals, the greater the likelihood that they will come through. If one of your goals is to buy a new car, be specific: what make, model, year, color, features, etc. So, write down as many goals as you can, be as specific as you can, and speak or declare all your goals as often as you can, or as often as practical in your situation, and choose three to five to focus on per day. This daily declaration is very important because we create with the power of our tongue.

Another useful aid in declaring goals, especially if you're visually inclined, is to create a vision board that contains images or symbols representing some of the things you want, especially the most important ones. Reviewing your vision board regularly can keep those goals fresh in the front of your mind, which will help you focus and set your priorities to ensure that your stairstep or secondary goals are truly serving your bigger purpose and vision. It will help you create an anchor into a reality for something in your subconscious that has not yet been created.

One powerful way to visualize your goals, especially the three to five goals you focus on each day, is to act them out, as in a play. Create a scenario in which you envision yourself walking into the reality of your goal. I know this may sound strange, but bear with me. Several years ago, I attended a personal development workshop where we created goals for five and ten years down the road, and then acted them out in small groups. One of my goals was to create a business that teaches people how to trade the stock market and have at least one client who made over $100,000 USD because of the education they received. Another goal was to get married, and another, to have children. Seven years later, every single goal that I acted out in that workshop came to pass and I am now living in the reality that I once portrayed in faith. Had I role-played them sooner, I might have achieved them sooner. In some of the workshops we hold with Neos, I help facilitate this life-changing method, and we have seen tremendous results come from it!

This brings up the importance of the role of our imagination in making our goals and declarations. As adults, we

> **Imagination creates a reality for us to step into.**

tend to think that imagination and play are frivolous or even a waste of time, and something that children engage in that help their growth and development. Imagination is much more than that, and we need it just as much as adults as when we were children, and perhaps more. In fact, Albert Einstein said, "Your imagination is everything. It is the preview of life's coming attractions." George Bernard Shaw said, "Imagination is the beginning of creation." What Imagination creates a reality for us to step into. It is a "dress rehearsal" for a future reality. When we use our imagination properly, we're actually role-playing for our future. How many times have you heard about a person who played doctor a lot as a child, and then grew up and became a doctor, or one who, as a child, sang on their living room table, and became a singer or an actor when they grew up? Our subconscious doesn't know the difference between role play and imagination versus reality. When we actually act out our imagination, we are in dress rehearsal for the future that we're going to step into. And one day soon, it will be "opening night," and the curtain will rise.

Another word for imagination is *visualization*. For example, every athlete who competes at a high level visualizes what they want to do. And they do it over and over and over again, in great detail. A close friend of mine helped train Olympic gold medalist Chad le Clos. He was a South African swimmer who won gold in the 200m butterfly in the 2012 Olympics by beating Michael Phelps. She told me that a large part of his training was visualizing every single stroke of the race before ever actually getting into the water. If he jumped off the block wrong, he started over. Every move, every stroke, was examined, analyzed, and corrected, with perfection as the goal. Everything was visualized over and over, and practiced over and over, until it was planted in the subconscious mind—the visualization of doing it perfectly. In order to win gold, this is what it takes. Then, when he was on the block and in his stance, when he launched out, his subconscious mind triggered, and he entered the water perfectly. It's the exact same for us. Essentially, it's not so much muscle memory as mind memory. Your body follows what your mind dictates. More proof of this concept is another former Olympian, Marilyn King. King said that after injuring her back in a car wreck that left her bed-ridden for a time, she used "mental rehearsal" or visualization to train. Without ever training on a track, she competed in the US Olympic trials and placed second!

Another important aspect of goals and declarations is learning to focus our energies into our goals. We all have different types of energies that we use every day. There is physical energy, which allows us to move around and work and play. People who are always moving, always busy, always going here and there, we say have "a lot of energy." The key to making our physical energy work for us is to learn how to focus it where it will help us the most in declaring and achieving our goals. Then there's emotional energy, which is tied to the huge waves of emotion that we all experience, sometimes on a daily basis. That, too, is an energy we can learn to focus. Sexual energy is another kind of energy we all possess, which is designed to literally create new life. I think we all understand the importance of properly focusing that energy. There are other energies present in us, but you get the idea.

All of these energies have creative parts to them. What I have found is that throughout the day, when you're wanting to focus on those three to five daily goals to declare, the best and most impactful time to declare those goals is when those moments of different energies hit us. Moments of high energy are the best time for declaring goals.

How does this work in practice? Let's take emotional energy, for example. Great joy and euphoria, as well as great sadness, generate a lot of emotional energy. I like to imagine myself taking it from where that energy is coming from. Most of our emotional energy comes either from our heart or our mind. I imagine myself releasing that energy behind my goals, almost like using it as a fuel, like a rocket engine. With sexual energy, which is an obvious creative energy, I imagine myself pulling that energy up and then releasing it out into my goals. With physical energy, I see myself pushing or pulling those goals into me. Then there's spiritual energy and imagining the releasing of our aura into our goals. It's a matter of learning to utilize those moments of heightened energy in our lives and focusing them with strength and intensity to help create the goals and the realities that we want to step into.

Too often we go through our goals almost mechanically. It is possible to simply repeat declarations so often without much thought that they drain us of energy rather than fire us up. We may declare, "By the time I'm forty years old, I'll have a liquid net worth of five million plus dollars." Okay, but there's nothing behind it. There's no energy involved. However, when we have those extreme energies focused, we can channel them into our goals to keep them alive in our mind and heart. This creates more substance around them bringing them closer to manifestation at every declaration! Learn to take control of your frustrations and use them to help propel you forward rather than hold you back. You have to learn how to control your emotions but not allow frustration to set you back; instead, learn to channel it so that it creates a positive force in your life. Focusing our energies effectively like this takes time to learn...and a lot of practice. But it's well worth the effort. When that happens consistently, and in conjunction with the six "keys" of giving, gratitude, new thinking, new hearing, faith, and stewardship, we will soon see our declared goals manifest in our lives. The Matthew Effect will become active in our lives; hacking the Pareto Distribution will become reality for us.

> **Learn to take control of your frustrations and use them to help propel you forward rather than hold you back.**

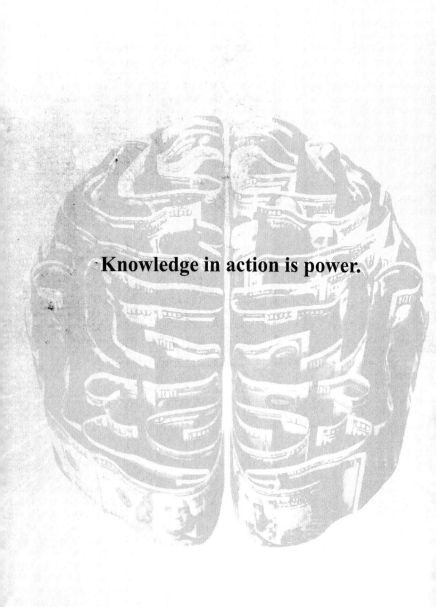

Knowledge in action is power.

Chapter Nine

Activating the Matthew Effect in Your Life

We have all heard the adage that "knowledge is power," and while I fully believe this is true, I would like to amend it slightly by saying that knowledge *in action* is power. Meaning, knowing something is not enough to take advantage of it. For example, I know that if I flip a switch on my wall, a light will turn on. However, the light will not turn on until I take the proper action, which is flipping that particular switch. The same is true of the Matthew Effect. While you now know that it is a spiritual law written into the fabric of this earth that was created to help you increase in wealth, knowing about it is not enough to have it work on your behalf. You must begin engaging it, you must take action, you must 'flip the switch' as it were, to see the increase it can bring into your life. Remember, you don't have to be great to get started, but you have to get started to become great.

In this final chapter, I want to encourage you to begin engaging this principle by offering you some simple ideas so that these spiritual keys can unlock the exponential growth the Matthew Effect can bring into your life. Let's begin by looking at each key one final time.

The first key we mentioned is the key of giving. This is our foundational starting point for having this law work on our behalf. Jesus himself said, "Give and it shall be given unto you, pressed down, shaken together, running over, shall men give into your bosom" (Luke 6:38 KJV). I know some of you may think, I don't have much to give at the end of every month, but remember what you DO have to give and the different 'floors' you can give to. Maybe you don't have a lot of finances left over, but you have time. Consider volunteering at a local homeless shelter where you can help serve food, vacuum or clean the building, do whatever they need done. Maybe you do have enough finances where buying a few canned goods wouldn't set you back too much. Then donate that food to a food pantry. If you want to do something really big, you could consider STARTING a canned food drive, blanket drive, or clothing drive where you then donate all of the goods to a local shelter or give to the poor and destitute. You can offer to help an elderly widow with some household chores or yard services, or just keep her company. Consider, if you have relationship with them, inviting them over for dinner. The key is remembering what you *DO* have available to give. We all have time, energy, and the ability to

Do not discount what you have, but plant it, speak blessings over it, and watch the increase the Lord brings into your life.

serve others in some capacity. Remember, a great forest starts with a single seed. Do not discount what you have, but plant it, speak blessings over it, and watch the increase the Lord brings into your life.

This leads us to the second key, which is gratitude. Rather than saying you don't have anything to offer, be thankful that you do have something to offer. Again, maybe you have the gift of administration, and you can help administrate the projects of giving mentioned above. Be thankful for that opportunity. Studies have been done proving that if we speak and bless plants as they grow, they grow better and produce tastier fruit. How much more will we grow and produce fruit if we are thankful and bless ourselves. Another great scripture for this is where Jesus is talking about judging. He says in Matthew 12:37, "For by your words you will be justified, and by your words you will be condemned" (NKJV). One meaning of this is that our words will be proven right. A great way to create a culture of gratitude in your life is to "count your wins" with your family or friends each day. What I mean by this is go over or send a list of your top three wins to someone who will push you toward your goals—like a spouse. Another great idea is to make a list of what you are thankful for and begin your day by declaring that list: "God, today I am thankful for my health, that I have a job, that the sun came up." Start as small or basic as you need to and watch that list grow. This simple step will begin to change the energy with which you approach your day and bring more opportunities to be thankful into your life. Remember, gratitude multiplies what you already possess! So, be thankful for the little: "I'm thankful I can pay my bills. I'm thankful I have a car to drive to work. I'm thankful I live in abundance." Begin doing this and then watch how what you have continues to grow into more and more.

> **Gratitude multiplies what you already possess!**

The third to engage is the key of new thinking. What is great about this key, is that if you practice the two prior keys, this new thinking will begin to be activated in your life. Most of us are not taught to live a lifestyle of giving and gratitude. If you start doing that, it will begin to transform the way you think. The easiest and best way to start this process is making "I am" statements about who you WANT to become. Do you want to be a millionaire? Then declare, "I am a millionaire with a net worth of two million dollars." If you want to see financial opportunities, then declare, "I am one who can see financial opportunity as it first presents itself." You can create these "I AM" statements with anything or any aspect you are wanting to step into in your life. One way to do this is take a washable marker (dry erase works too) and write your "I AM" statement on your bathroom mirror. Then, when you see them, say them. The more energy you can use, the better it will be. Another easy-to-do step is to begin reading (or listening to) books that challenge your mindset on money. Take a class on trading or investing in the stock market. Because you are one of our readers, my wife and I would like to offer you our first course "Zero to Trading" for 30 percent off with coupon code MATTHEWEFFECT at checkout. I have all of the instructions to take advantage of this opportunity on our resources page. Also on our resources page, I have compiled a list of our favorite, most impactful books that pertain to having a wealth mindset. I would highly encourage you to visit the resources page in the back of this book and begin reading some of the books on that list. I would tell you to start with "Think and Grow Rich" or "Rich Dad Poor Dad." Those are classics when it comes to mindset adjustments around money. If you are serious about this journey, reading is one of the best ways to help change your mindset. Another key is to surround yourself with positive people who think in terms of success. There is an old saying: "If you hang out with four millionaires, chances are you will be the fifth!" Look for and even pray for people to come into your life that challenge you to attain higher levels of success and call out the greatness in you. This isn't always easy to do but can be helpful. Oftentimes, it happens naturally that as we change and grow, those around us don't and, as a result, we go our separate ways. Also on the resources page, we have some teachings that will help you create healthy boundaries and relationships by some of our trusted friends.

I believe that the fourth key of the Matthew Effect, which is changing the way we hear, is a byproduct of changing the way we think. When we are making declarations, reading and engaging our mind with new principals, and surrounding ourselves with more positive and influential people, we automatically start hearing things differently.

The fifth key to this is faith. Please remember that faith first comes by hearing. That's it, nothing more. I believe (because I have experienced) that when we hear ourselves release positive affirmations and declarations over our own lives, and when we hear those around us encourage and inspire us to greatness, this faith grows naturally for us to believe it. While you may start declaring your goals with doubt in your heart, eventually you begin to believe it and a conscious choice takes over to create a tree of faith in your life. Jesus says "The kingdom of heaven is like a mustard seed, which a person took and sowed in his field; and this is smaller than all the other seeds, but when it is fully grown, it is larger than the garden plants and becomes a tree, so that the birds of the sky come and nest in its branches" (Matt13:31-32). There is a mystery here that I don't have time to go into, but I can tell you that the small seed you begin to declare will grow and the faith for it will grow until it manifests in your life. Another key element of *TRUE* faith requires action. James puts it this way, "Faith without works is dead." (James 2:20). So, put some life into your declarations and take action. Start a new course on trading, investing, or real-estate, open a new business, look into doing something to have your faith put into action!

The sixth and final key is stewardship. How well you steward these principles in your life will determine how far and how well they will work for you. If you only engage them for a few months, they will only work for you for a few months. However, if you create a lifestyle of living out these concepts, I can promise that you will manifest a life of growing, abundance, and prosperity. Albert Einstein once said, "Compound interest is the eighth wonder of the world, he who understands it, earns it; he who doesn't, pays for it." If you steward well over these keys, this principle will begin to compound for you and the generations that follow. Don't give up, only believe. Have faith, for your future is bright! The plans the Lord has for you are plans to prosper you, to give you hope and a future (Jer 29:11) in this life and beyond. I want to encourage you to practice and not give up. Continue to pursue these keys and watch the Matthew Effect propel you forward. I hope you have enjoyed this book, and I would love to hear how it has impacted your life. Make sure to visit the resources page in the back of the book to contact us for more information.

To learn more about some of the topics mentioned above, we recommend reading the following books.

Books on Mindset
- Think and Grow Rich – Napoleon Hill
- If How To's Were Enough – Brian Klemmer
- Rich Dad Poor Dad – Robert Kiyosaki
- Secrets of the Millionaire Mind – T Harv Eker
- Atomic Habits - James Clear

Books on Relationship & Character
- Weaponized Honor – Marios Ellinas (Giving)
- Tables and Platforms – Marios Ellinas

- Can't Hurt Me – David Goggins
- How to Win Friends and Influence People – Dale Carnegie
- The 5 Love Languages – Gary Chapman
- Keep Your Love On – Danny Silk

Books on Goal Setting
- The Magic of Thinking BIG – David Schwartz
- 7 Habits of Highly Effective People – Stephen Covey
- Who Are You Really And What Do You Want – Shad Helmstetter

Books on Trading & Investing
- Trading in the Zone - Mark Douglas
- The Disciplined Trader - Mark Douglas
- One Good Trade – Mike Bellafiore

Now that you've finished reading *Understanding the Matthew Effect*, I'd appreciate it if you would leave your honest review on the Amazon listing. It will help other readers find the best book for them too.

Also, send me an email with any questions or feedback you have regarding this material: mwilburn@neoscdg. com

Products and Services

Mark and his wife, Kate, teach the principles in this book through courses and subscriptions offered by their company NEOS Capital Development Group, as well as in person through speaking events and workshops. There are several options to dig deeper for yourself individually or for a more corporate setting.

Speaking & Workshops

Invite Mark and Kate to speak at your next event. At our live speaking events we help facilitate change in people lives by empowering them with teachings and activations on:

- How to determine your goals and dreams, discover what is keeping you from engaging them, create an atmosphere for them to manifest in your life.
- How to identify and overcome toxic mindsets around money, finances, wealth, and investing.
- How to identify and overcome toxic mindsets around relationships so that you can be a better spouse, parent, friend, and leader.
- How to apply biblical financial principles that manifest results in the natural, not just spiritual.

NEOS Capital Development Group—Trading & Investing Education

Where other trading education programs focus solely on "getting rich quick," at NEOS we focus on creating generational wealth. What legacy will you leave?

We do not manage your money, we teach YOU how to do it.

Creating wealth transcends the bank account, which can be an enlightening experience; this is what gives life to our motto "we trade on a different floor." At NEOS, we believe that "trading on a different floor" has a multi-dimensional meaning, the most obvious one being at the actual New York Stock Exchange, which represents the physical location where trades take place. We also believe that there are more spiritual trading floors. A floor, in this sense, can be as simple as WHERE you sow/give/trade your resources; or more ethereal in nature. As you elevate yourself and your legacy with NEOS education, our hope is that you experience with us benefits every facet of life.

Visit us at www.neoscdg.com and use coupon code MATTHEWEFFECT for 30 percent off our Zero to Trading Course. Simply add the course to your shopping cart, enter the coupon code & hit apply.

Some of what we offer:

Core Trading Courses:

1. **Zero to Trading** – Built with the beginner in mind, our foundational course to trading and investing in the stock market will take you from zero experience to having the confidence needed to trade in the stock market for yourself.

2. **Options Unfolded** – Learn how to find, select, trade, and manage the proper option in order to leverage your trading decisions using options.

3. **Escalating Education: Debit Spreads** – Learn how this strategy can increase your probability of making profits using options rather than stocks. This is a great way for smaller accounts to engage and trade higher dollar stocks.

4. **Escalating Education: Credit Spreads** – Learn one of the highest probability trades that you can take when it comes to option trading. This strategy is critical for any trader who hopes to make consistent profits when trading in the market.

Course Packages:

- Silver Package
- Gold Package

Additional Trading Courses/Strategies:

- Plus Additional Trading Courses/Strategies

Mindset Trainings:

- Activate: Better Mindset, Better Results

Supportive Subscription-based Products:

- Tiered Memberships
  - Foundational
  - Enhanced
  - Premier
- Ready. Set. Trade.

About the Author

Mark, along with his wife Kate, is the owner and operator of NEOS Capital Development Group, and partnering businesses. The central focus of NEOS is to provide education to help increase people's returns on their investments as they pertain to the stock market.

Mark has two Bachelor's degrees in Marketing and Real Estate and over twelve years experience as a trading consultant and trainer. At NEOS, he is the head trainer and empowers people by taking them from a baseline knowledge level and giving them tools, strategies, understanding, and confidence to, potentially, be able to become a successful trader themselves.

Mark is passionate about teaching principles that breach the borders of "finance" and address economic laws that have been coded into creation itself. He firmly believes not only in recognizing the greatness in others, but empowering them with knowledge and opportunity to step into that greatness for themselves.

He currently resides in Georgia with his wife, Kate, and their four sons, Maverick, Blaze, Phoenix, and Zephaniah.

CAPITAL DEVELOPMENT GROUP

www.neoscdg.com

support@neoscdg.com

833-636-7234

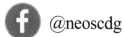 @neoscdg

 @neoscdg1

 @neoscdg